Months and Days

Titus Naso

Tomis Press

Months and Days
Titus Naso

Published by Tomis Press
Silverton, Oregon

Hardcover ISBN: 978-1-958337-05-9
Paperback ISBN: 978-1-958337-20-2
E-Book ISBN: 978-1-958337-21-9

Titus Naso is a pen name of Jesse S. Smith.

titusnaso.com • tomispress.com • jessesmithbooks.com

Poetry / History / Society and Culture

Introduction

At the height of the Covid-19 pandemic lockdowns early in the year 2020, I was reading Ovid's *Fasti*, a collection of poems about the Roman calendar and holidays. Inspired by Ovid's work, I challenged myself to write a poem a day for the next year.

This book of the year is a selection of the poems written during that year, rounded out with minor later additions. The poems in this collection commemorate our favorite cultural celebration days, recall the history of the names of the months of our modern calendar, and ponder the holy days of the ancients.

Try skipping forward to today's date, or your birthday, or your favorite holiday, and see what you find. Have fun with it.

May all your days be merry!

~Titus Naso
March 31, 2022

January

New Year's Day
1-1-21

Today at last a New Year has begun,
it is the time we all get a fresh start.
We shall go forth in search of joy and fun
and try to put some gladness in our hearts.
With each New Year our lives begin again
symbolic'ly, marked with resolutions.
We tell ourselves that we'll improve by then,
inner lives undergo revolutions.
A time of change is a time to improve,
it's such a time when calendar renews.
We can decide to fill the world with love,
we can decide to be the selves we choose.
We stride t'wards hope ahead, leave fears behind,
and hope to control destiny with our minds.

Perihelion
1-2-21

Elliptical the path we hurtle 'round
about the Sun, as Earth revolves through space:
not circular, elongated orbit
brings us sometimes closer to our home star
and sometimes out in space farther away.
Today's the day of Perihelion:
a special day, as astronomers know,
for on this day we're closer to the Sun
than any other day throughout the year
by some three million miles in outer space –
tremendous distance in our human terms,
yet hardly noticed on galactic scale
and on our seasons it has no effect:
they are caused by rotating axis tilt.
Thus we approach the Sun in winter cold,
but strength within ourselves will make us bold.

Janus
1-3-21

With praises to Janus the year begins,
the two-faced god (just like a two-faced friend)
who looks ahead and also sees behind:
the guardian of doorways, and of change.
With celebration Rome greeted the year,
and in procession to the temple walked;
new magistrate in carved palanquin sat;
great bulls were sacrificed, people did feast.
God Janus with symbolic staff and key
appeared to Ovid (in the eye of mind)
and claimed he had been "Chaos" to the Greeks,
primordial force from which all else descends!
The guardian he remains of Universe,
presiding over season's change, and times.
Ovid explains, the Winter Solstice marks
the time when each New Year has fresh begun
(although by convention historical
 relating to the lunar calendar,
 ten days have gone by before the New Year).

Inauguration Day: A Limerick
(Once every four years on January 20)

Hooray! Inauguration Day – rejoice!
In joyous song together lift our voice.
    And if your party lost,
     just keep your fingers crossed:
in four years you will get another choice!

Orion
1-21-21

Thou, recognizable constellation
so large, glowing in the winter night sky,
in earliest mythic stories mentioned art.
Orion! With thy belt and dangling sword,
a figure most imposing to the eye,
you stand up tall when summer says goodbye.
Traditions naming thee must ancient be,
for once remembered, who'd forget thy name?
The hunter! Archètype so masculine,
those first-named stars a star did represent:
to people long ago a folk hero,
the mighty hunter men aspired to be.

Likely predating the Olympian gods,
the later storytellers him despised,
provincial and barbaric Orion;
thus stories they invented about him:
disgusting origin and deeds most fell,
the hero's downfall and his just disgrace.

Yet later centuries, the poets great
his myth revived, and gave a brand-new spin
to stories of Orion the Hunter.

The First Month
1-4-21

From Roman Janus "January" derives,
this month which is the doorway to the year.
We enter 'pon this new time in our lives
and flip the finger at our ling'ring fear.
Since ancient times this month have Hebrews named
the month of Tevet, lunar cycle ten.
In ancient Egypt, this periòd same
was known as Tybi, in those days back then.
For Old English traditions glad I am,
and they called this month "Yule," just like the last;
whereas this was once the month of the ram
(per Snorri) to the Old Norse of the past.
But ancient Macedon leaves me confused:
was Eudymios, or Audmaios, the name they used?

The Feast of the Epiphany
1-6-21

When twelve days more have passed since Christmas morn
and all the "lords-a-leaping" have been sung,
we celebrate Epiphany's feast day!
Still called Theophany in th' ornate East,
'tis said this was the day Three Wise Men came,
Kings Balthazar, Caspar, and Melchior,
from following a star to Bethlehem,
and found there, in a manger filled with hay,
a baby, fast asleep in that cold barn;
and to his mother these Three Wise Men sang praise,
and told her that she'd given birth to God,
and she said that made sense, coz God was Dad.
Then all the shepherds sang, and angels too,
as to this mother those Wise Men gave gifts
of gold, and frankincense, and precious balms.
And Mary thanked them graciously, although
perhaps a blanket might have been preferred!

Treason Day
1-6-21.ii

This Treason Day goes down in infamy,
and ever after shall remembered be.

Doing the bidding of the "President"
who holds himself above the law, always,
extremist supporters of Donald Trump
on this day stormed the Capitol Building
in Washington, D.C. – no mere protest,
it was an act of violent rebellion!
The Joint Chambers were into hiding forced,
prevented from confirming vote tally.

They do not believe in democracy.
They told us all along they'd not accept
election results, unless their guy won –
it's no surprise that they would not accept
election results, after their guy lost.

No peace or freedom would satisfy them –
they want democracy quite overthrown!
They have always preferred dictatorship,
they made that clear almost six years ago.

Inciting rioters to Congress storm
in hopes of preventing election loss
was quite in keeping with Trump's character.
It is exactly who he's always been:
a wannabe Augustus Emperor.

This was a low point for America:
may we all learn from our mistakes henceforth,
resolving to do better evermore.
Our peaceful transfer is what makes us great –
we still can save it; it is not too late.

Agonalia
1-9-21

The Agonalia thrice each year was held:
you'll also find it May the 21st.
'Twas on December 11 as well,
a date not included in Ovid's verse.
The ritual of sacrificial blood
is one that from our culture now is gone.
There was a time when all thought it was good,
and knife-wielding priest asked, "Do I go on?"
In early days, folks thought it was enough
to make a sacrifice of salt and spelt;
but as Rome grew, folks wanted to be tough:
the need for extra blood and gore was felt.
A sow for Ceres, or for Jove a bull;
for Mars a goat or ram, then feast until you're full!

The Ritual of Sacrifice
1-10-21

Long has the ritual of sacrifice
associated been with worship good –
by making off'rings to the gods, people
ensured good fortune in the days to come.
Sometimes the gods demanded the whole thing,
sometimes they were content with nasty guts,
depending on the culture and the time.
In his creative catalog of days,
the outcast poet recalls some he's seen
and tales of how tradition was begun:
people of old, it seems, held strange ideas
that hives of bees would generate themselves
spontaneously from a dead bull carcass
(but good Lucretius knew better than that).

The Romans sacrificed the sheep and ox,
the Persians to Hyperion gave a horse,
to Artemis the Grecians gave a doe,
and offered up a donkey, famed for dick,
in sacrifice to Priapus the dick,
whose boner graced the gardens of the Greeks
to scare away the birds, and robbers, too.
And at Idalium was a white dove sacrificed,
perhaps to Venus? And in Rome a goose
to Isis, goddess of far Egypt's Nile,
was on an altar holy sacrificed;
and Nox, goddess of Night, to whom a bird,
an unnamed, crested noisy morning bird
(a crested fowl) was offered up to take
revenge symbolic for shatt'ring the night's
beloved stillness: but which crested bird?
a rooster? peacock? hoopoe? It's unclear!
And Ovid says he's seen in his exile
the tribespeople of Thrace on the Black Sea
as far as snowy slopes of Mt. Haemus,
who sacrificed a dog to Hecate,
the goddess of Moon magic and strange charms
who guarded over crossroads and changes –
Sapaean priests did open up that dog,
pull out its guts, and on the altar burn
them as an offering to Hecate
who was formidable to Hesiod.
When we look back on this from our vantage,
we think such customs are so strange and quaint;
and yet even today we recognize
sometimes to gain we must give something up.

Plough Monday
1-11-21

Parades sometimes still celebrate
    the Monday of the Plough,
for work down on the charming farm
    can be resumèd now.

It's not so common any more
    for Bessy and the Fool
to parade, as in days of yore,
    with the furrowing tool.

Musicians played, and dancers danced,
    in procession down the street.
Bystanders laughed and stood entranced
    when this strange group they'd meet.

Tho fields be cold and mornings chill
    there can be no excuse:
hard work is ploughing, even still –
    put this day to good use!

Evander
1-12-21

He's clearly sympathetic as he tells
the tale of Evander, who was exiled;
but Ovid's sympathy to his subject
perhaps has blinded him to the details.
For as Ovid relates the narrative
presented as a goddess' prophecy,
we hear the goddess Carmentis describe
the exile of Evander in terms
that might be quest'nable, subjectively.

She tells the hero king, "It's not your fault,
  some god was offendèd, as gods are wont;
  you could not have avoided such a fate,
  it did not matter what you might have done!"
It turns out, he'd murdèred his father. Oh!
And tho his mother'd asked him to do it,
perhaps the gods had reason for their rage,
and Ovid's sympathy might be misplaced.

The Republic's End
1-13-21

'Twas on this day the Roman Senators
bestowed the title of Augustus to
their Emperor, at the Republic's end,
and with great celebrations they all cheered
the man whose army ended Civil War
(tho he himself was sickly and fought not).

Carmentis
1-15-21

'Tis strange, the tale Ovid tells of this day:
it would have been transgressive in his time.
The royal women, when they had conceived,
their fetuses aborted by blunt force
to protest loss of carriage conveyance
which previously had been their privìlege.
Their husbands, so alarmed by this outrage,
restored the carriages to their wild wives.
We're not told how this episode began,
or what it has to do with Carmentis.
Because of it, her temple has two days
of mystic rituals to honor her –
the first, three days ago; the next, today:

the first, the masculine; this, feminine.
The rites call out goddesses from afar,
Porrima and Postverta, èxaltèd
companions of the prophetess goddess...
but Ovid seems unint'rested in them.
No leather in the temple may be worn:
only the living doth Carmentis love!
Keep altars pure as her, goddess above.

Religious Freedom Day
January 16

Religious Freedom Day has been proclaimed,
this day of January, the sixteenth,
to celebrate the Virginian statute
eventually incorporated into
the First Amendment of the Constitution.
We all are free to follow our own hearts,
and no one can tell us what to believe!

Concordia
1-16-21

From conquest was derived the wealth of Rome,
from plundered spoils of war, tribute brought home.
Expansion drove their growth economy
with riches, slaves, and new territory.
Their temples grand and living standards high
were built from wars when innocents must die.
The ire of enemies by this outrage
was so inflamed, it ended Roman age.
In retrospect, we know this irony
when we look back on Roman history;
and on us irony must not be lost
when we hear how those wars paid for the cost
of building up Concordia's temple grand
to honor peace and love throughout the land.

A dictator first promised to the crowd,
"A temple will be built!" Furius vowed
to bring the working class back from boycott
when they the city left in one big lot
reminding the wealthy what the poor brought:
"We do your work, respect you have forgot,
  and since like shit you treat us, ev'ry hour,
  we're leaving you to demonstrate our pow'r!"
Their story may be the best I have told yet,
vox populi magnus, let us not forget!

Martin Luther King Day
The Third Monday in January

O for to "Love thy neighbor as thyself,"
"Love thine enemy," "Turn the other cheek,"
O for the search for peace within oneself
despite critics who love to call us "weak."
O for the spread of love unto the poor
O for a love that can transcend all race
O let us each realize we can do more
and do our work with smiles upon our face.
This was the message preached by Dr. King,
a message we recall upon this day –
a man who dared to dream the futur'd bring
that universal love for which we pray.
So on this day let us recall his dream,
that equal rights may in the future gleam.

Wise Istros, lover, poet, satirist,
imagined Artemis falling in love
with that great hunter who her talents matched.
Her jealous brother, Apollo the god,
did trick her into shooting her lover:
she thought it target practice, loosed the shaft.
As lightning from the hand of Zeus it sped
so swiftly that it struck him in the head.
To shore his corse it drifted, and she shrieked
in horror when she saw what she had done.

But Ovid to the Scorpion's deadly sting
attributes violent death and sky placement:
our hero leapt bravely to the defense
of Leto, and he was stung in her stead –
tho 'twas his fault, in fact, for Gaea sent
his murd'rer to protect the creatures wild
from his excessive zeal – he'd kill them all!
An early indication this may be
that hunting out of season was taboo.
The management of wildlife is a trust,
and we must be responsible, and think
so all the creatures wild might thrive and grow
and we might live as one with Mother Earth.

Sowing Day
1-23-21

A Sowing Day the Romans did proclaim
upon that season's day when seed was sown,
the land receptive to the farming rites.
Bright garlands hung in wreaths on oxen strong
and ye may rest who've tilled and sown the earth.
A holiday farmers did celebrate
and stroll from house to house with joy to share.
They to their neighbors gave the cakes of spelt
in honor of Ceres, goddess of grain;
and to her, cattle sacrifice was made.

May fragile sprouts to seedlings strong well grow
may fields untroubled by cold late snow be
May gentle rains and warming sun give grace,
may birds and herds stay clear of fresh-tilled fields
May golden grains grow strong, from mildew free,
not withering, and neither over-bold.
May fields be free of weeds, may crops grow tall
May Earth be fertile and reward thy work
May warriors to ploughshares beat their swords,
and mattocks make in place of javelins.
May we our efforts turn to harmony
and nurture Peace, O Ceres, nurture Peace,
as we nurture the Peace that nurtures thee.

The Feast of the Conversion of St. Paul
1-25-21

One of the greatest Christian saints
    was once a sinner, too!
He made mistakes not small, but great,
    yes, just like me and you.

In the employ of conquerors
    to heretics prosecute,
Saul did what he had always done –
    'twas no forbidden fruit.

He rode the road one winter day
    when revelation struck –
described he "like a lightning bolt"
    it came as such a shock.

Then to the ground he senseless fell
    as though he'd been struck blind,
while thoughts of all the wrongs he'd done
    waged war within his mind.

The Bible contradicts itself
    whether his companions heard.
We understand it's metaphor
    when "heaven" spoke those words.

But sure it is, his life he changed,
    he turned it all around:
his job, his game, even his name
    from that event profound.

As Paul, he framed his message new
    and preached it to the masses,
'bout how his life had turned around
    while riding t'wards Damascus.

Too bad the Christians did not learn
    from old Saint Paul's mistakes:
they Jews and Mithraists did burn,
    and "witches," at the stake.

Pax

1-30-21

May Peace reign in our lives, may we have Peace –
not like the peace of terror that was brought
to Rome after Octavian won the war
at Actium, when his naval flotilla
defeated Antony and Cleopatra,
that shameful day when Antony lost faith
and fled the fight to follow Egypt's queen,
abandoning his forces to their fate.
That's not the peace we crave, no peace of shame:
but neither do we relish thoughts of war –
at least, not those of us who've thought it through!

We pray for seasoned Peace, a peace that lasts,
a peace that settles in our bones and stays,
a peace to build our livelihood around,
that we may raise our fam'lies and grow old,
that businesses may prosper, and our crops
not army-trampled, nor watered with blood,
grow strong with fertilizer and with sun;
the gentle rains sustain the harvest good
which will sustain us through the winter-time.
O gentle Peace, keep enemies at bay,
let glory and success through Peace be found.
There is no need to seek out battle death;
we can together work to strengthen Peace.
We shall stay vigilant, defenses man,
attacks and hostile threats we shall stave off,
'til keeping Peace shall be a glory great
and all praise leaders' names who keep the Peace.
Whether through love of us or fear of us,
let enemies avoid conflict of arms
and only us engage in fights of words.
Let us compete in sports, and business too,
let us compete to throw parties more grand,
let us compete to be healthy and wise,
let us complete, yet keep an open hand;
let us compete yet light our eyes with love.

New Year's Resolutions
1-31-21

Have you your New Year's Resolutions kept?
Or have you broken them all while you slept?
We are about to close the year's front door,
but do not worry, there's eleven more!

Did you your New Year's Resolutions break?
Perhaps there was not quite enough at stake.
But should you take good Janus as your friend,
the door will open for you once again.

February

Joe Soloy Day (Alaska)
February 1

Exploring boundless tracts of wilderness
his helicopter flew uncharted skies!
He tagged for study polar bears on ice.
He helped those engineers survey for roads,
and pipelines for the fuel that helped us grow.
A pilot, an explorer, fam'ly man,
a twentieth century pioneer.

Immolc
2-2-21

This holiday repurposed many times
has been, throughout the years, and new names giv'n.
It always celebrates the way sun shines
a little brighter in these days we're livin'.
Midway between Solstice and Equinox,
the Pagans named it Imbolc, when the ewes
began to birth new lambs, replenish stocks,
we celebrate the life that now ensues.
The Cath'lics, Pagan holiday then tamed,
but still they celebrated Sun's return
when Candlemas this day they did rename
and blessed the candles which through winter burned.
America made it sillièr still
with Groundhog Day, and Punxsutawney Phil!

Delphinus
2-3-21

Esteemed Sappho of Lesbos the most famed
musician, poet and lover renowned,
thy words resound down the millenia
tho thy voice long since has faded away.
Was Arion thy contemporary?
Didst thou know him? Hate him? Love him? Fuck him?
Did he sing of thee? Didst thou sing of him?
His tale has found its way to Ovid's pen,
this musical Arion you might know,
on February third, when at nighttime
the Dolphin constellation sets for Spring;
the Dolphin, perhaps friend t' Amphitrite,
mayhap savior of Arion and Lyre.
The tale told by Greek Eratosthenes
is of the former: wooing gone astray,
a strangely common theme in ancient myth.
But Hyginus, his Roman translator
(whose work may have been known to our Ovid)
appends the story that Ovid expounds,
a tale told by Herodotus also,
about the wand'ring minstrel Arion
who was beset aboard ship by the crew,
who held him hostage, demanding his wealth:
with sword in hand threatened to take his life!
But music has great pow'r over the world,
and in that power Arion trustèd:
he strummed his lyre, then dove into the waves,
where Delphinus the Dolphin, who had heard
the harp's sweet music, saved him, bore him up.
By dolphin saved from drowning, Arion
continued playing, as through ocean waves
the dolphin bore him safely back to shore.
But Hyginus (citing another source)
suggests as an *aetion* yet a third tale:
Dionysos, a boy for Naxos bound,

was under threat of shipboard kidnapping,
by those sailors who should have kept him safe.
They into dolphins were transformed instead,
a transformation Ovid too relates
in his most famous *Metamorphoses.*

O canst thou tell us which of these is true
great Sappho, singer talented and wise?
From which tale did star dolphin take its name,
or were these explanations added late?
If thou couldst tell us, we could learn so much!
We praise thee, Sappho, and for blessings pray.

Juno Sospita
2-4-21

Now fallen into disrepair, the shrine
of Sospita the Savior goddess grand
was on the first of February blessed
as multitudes did cheer her holy name.
O blessèd Juno, why did Rome forget
thy beauty and reconciliation?
Perhaps your skill in keeping peace at home
is what kept Rome away from your temple:
so warlike had their whole country become,
no longer did they value saving grace.
The shrine acquired a certain infamy
when drunken couples ducked insight at night
for a quick fuck in a darkened corner
(perhaps involving an exchange of funds)
displaying disregard for holiness.
By Ovid's time merely a pile of stones,
the ancient shrine collapsed into decay,
its roof and walls had fallen in disgrace,
a lack of love for thee, goddess of love.

Father of the Homeland
2-5-21

Had I a million voices, I'd want more:
to sing of gratitude, sorrow drown out,
from narratives of hatefulness distract.
O Rome, why didst thou fall wholeheartedly
under the sway of tyrants and madmen,
and praise them all the while, almost as though
a gracious favor they performed for thee
by absolute pow'r usurping to reign
and democratic government destroy?

'Twas on this day, the Senate title gave
of "Father of the Homeland" official
to Augustus the intolerant and cruel
who harshly judged but brooked no criticism –
in contrast stark to founding Romulus
whose sacred grove would welcome anyone,
as equals treat them no matter their past,
asylum grant without question of wrong;
for equal treatment of fellow humans
is surely the mark of a great leader.

Superbowl Sunday
2-7-21.ii

Today is Superbowl Sunday,
    kick that ball into the air!
Most Americans shout, "Hooray!"
    but I personally do not care.

Rome's First Day of Spring
2-10-21

'Twas on this day in ancient times, they say,
as reckoned were the days of season's change,
the Spring began. O, joy and glory, Spring!
Although Ovid cautions the reader wise,
as glitt'ring Lucifer the Morning Star
doth bring his light to shine upon the waves,
that cold remains, yes, lingers winter's chill.

The Second Month
2-11-21

From Ovid's poetry we learn, the month
of February takes its ancient name
from th' Latin word for purification,
a word already ancient by his time.
To back up his assertion, he relates
that priests in charge of ritual most high
would ask the highest priest for woolen tufts
which were called by the name of *februa*.
The houses of the priests were cleansed as well
with rituals of roasted spelt and salt,
which also had the name of *februa*.
The word must have referred to implements
of rituàl cleaning and purity.
The same word, Ovid goes on to explain,
described a pine tree branch of purity,
as he himself had seen in rituals,
concluding that the word was widely used
in ref'rence to objects which purify,
and had done so since all men went unshaved.
But why then is the month known by this name?
It seems Ovid is not entirely sure:
because this is the Lupercalia month
when priests who honor Faunus purify
the ground with rituals of leather straps;

or else because Feralia festival
remembèring the honored dead with feasts
did purify the whole year that followed.
One often finds when Ovid choices gives,
the one he presents last is likeliest.
Although he does not argue preference,
it seems that Ovid favored this latter,
associating *februa* with death.

As scholarly Bēdē discovered since,
there prob'ly was a good reason for this:
there was an ancient god named Februus,
who likely was for Pluto a cognate;
a god of riches, purity, and death,
a god of the Etruscan pantheon,
predating the culture of ancient Rome
by sev'ral hundred years or perhaps more
until they were conquered and assimilated.
Th' Etruscans were Rome's neighbors since always,
their cultures surely shared a common bond,
their languages based on a common root.
From this it seems clear that we may conclude
our month of February takes its name
from purity conferred by sacrifice
to an ancient god of death named Februus.

Old lunar calendars approximate
the month of February, Bēdē writes.
The ancient Hebrews named this month Shevat,
eleventh in their lunar calendar.
The Old English called this month Solmonath,
(a name that clearly has a Latin root)
in honor of the lengthening of days
just like the Christian day of Candlemas,
although Bēdē translates it "month of cakes"
after the cakes folks baked about this time,
just like those cakes of spelt Ovid described.
We learn from Snorri, this month was Thorri
in ancient Nordic lands of ice and snow

perhaps to honor Mjolnir's wielder strong.
In ancient Macedon, Peritios
is what they called this month in books of lore.
In Egypt with their solar calendar
and mighty Pharaohs who built pyramids
with slaves and stones and engineering feats,
they numbered this month sixth; its name, Mecheir.
The meaning of some names is lost to us,
the beauty of our shared culture is not;
for they, as we, did number out their days
in trying to bring order to their lives.

Chinese New Year
2-12-21

In China, the New Year begins today,
the grandest celebration of the year,
the day when Winter ends and Spring begins.
More than a billion people celebrate
with dragon dances, and meals with fam'ly,
with fancy decorations and fireworks.
With ritual house cleaning start anew,
and wish prosperity to your loved ones
with gifts of money in red envelopes.
Bright decorations are from paper cut
and on windows and doors couplets are hung
of pretty verses in the Chinese script.
Traditions ancient of solemnity
do blend with wild exuberance and joy
as in the sky the fireworks bright explode!
Symbolic cycle, twelve-year zodiac,
names this year the mighty Year of the Ox.
Approach your problems with a bull's great strength!
It is my fervent hope, yes most sincere,
that you'll enjoy a prosperous Chinese New Year!

Callisto
2-12-21.iii

Callisto was a nymph, as Ovid tells.
Until she was seduced by Jupiter,
she with Diana played – but belly swells
revealed shame. Said goddess, "Away with her!"
No longer could she be Hamadryad;
off sadly by herself Callisto went.
And let's be fair, though she'd done nothing bad,
Diana had in rage her away sent.
Soon Arcas was the babe from this affair,
but long before the boy e'er came of age
mad Juno turned Callisto to a bear,
for jealousy had quite filled her with rage.
One day much later, Arcas the bear would have killed!
They both were placed in stars before her blood was spilled.

Abraham Lincoln's Birthday
2-12-21.v

'Twas seven score and sixteen years ago
when he became a martyr to his cause.
The leader who brought slav'ry to an end
then gave his life for what he had achieved.

A rags-to-riches story; but it's true!
A boy who in a log cabin was raised
and taught himself from textbooks found in trash
succeeded in becoming someone great.
A lawyer, well-respected in his town,
he was elected to State government,
for four terms to the Illinois State House
before he was elected to a seat
of Fed'ral government, the U.S. House.
The prominence helped him spread his ideas
and drew attention to good Abraham.

A candidate of compromise he was:
'twas on the third ballot his name rose up.
Electors then chose Lincoln President!

But in the South, they had other ideas:
no compromise was possible with them.
From Union they most haughtily withdrew,
and fired the war's first shots on Fort Sumter.
Tho passive Lincoln had not this desired,
he understood his duties all too well
to country, liberty; to God and man;
and thus he chose the Union to defend
against the mad aggression of the South.

Th' Emancipation Proclamation did
grant freedom to the slaves across the South:
a late triumph for justice, with no teeth
given the state of war there at that time.
Thus liberty's progress imperfect is,
by fits and starts, backsliding and great grief,
yet nonetheless, we hold to our ideals!

An army raised and fought for four hard years
with devastating weapons. Much had changed,
and warfare's tactics lagged behind the times.
A hundred thousand died at Gettysburg
in just a single day of fighting there.
On back of envelope, riding the train,
Lincoln composed his most famous Address.

Equality became the law at last
in 1865, when ratified
Amendment the Thirteenth at last became.

The bloody Civil War ground to an end.
At Appomattox Gen'ral Lee gave in,
admitting that he had suffered defeat.

But Lincoln did not long survive the peace.
He went to see a play, and was gunned down.
We celebrate good Abraham today,
the man who brought an end to slavery
(although it had not been his object first).
His core belief that Union must prevail
has shaped these great United States today!

The Defeat of the Fabii
2-13-21.iv

So arrogantly the Romans marched out
to war, believing none could them defeat.
The ruling fam'ly of the Fabii
had gathered up an army of soldiers,
three hundred marched out of the city gates,
a small division by our modern terms,
intending neighbor Tuscans to attack.
The River Cremera was then in flood,
says Ovid, from the heavy winter rains.
And by its banks they pitched a camp, then charged!
Their rush pierced the Etruscan lines, men fled,
the Romans stabbed them in the back with glee.
Believing they had won the victory,
they jumped for joy to celebrate success.
Numerically superior Tuscans
did then regroup, surrounding Roman flanks.
Then Romans did regret flood at their back!
They had nowhere to go. They could not win.
Their arrogance was repaid with the sword.
Etruscans slaughtered Fabii that day,
and cut then down, yes, ev'ry single one,
allowing Roman blood so arrogant
to stain Cremera's flood a dirty red.

The Ides of February
2-13-21

In ancient Rome, the Ides was the Thirteenth
of February, as Ovid recounts;
the priests of Faunus on that day began
preparing rituals both raw and wild
in honor of the god of wilderness,
the Roman cognate of the rustic Pan.
The Lupercalia festival of fame
was two days later (by our reckoning)
on the 15th – 'twas quite a sight to see
the naked men with whips run through the streets
to bless the willing women as they watched,
fertility conferred with leather lash
upon the tender back of outstretched hand –
but let's not kid ourselves, there must have been
at times during that drunken festival
fertility conferred the usual way
around the corner, up against a wall
when nobody was looking, or at least
nobody who was really important.
The ancient poets tend to skip that part,
but surely it happened, so have a heart.
Thus ancient Lupercalia is the root of Valentine,
by Catholics appropriated and refined.

Valentine's Day
2-14-21

Through joys and trials we ever stronger grow!
Tho life brings many unexpected fears,
it is quite deeply comforting to know
that I can count on you throughout the years.
Life's journey such a grand adventure is
and always there's so much to see and do!
The magic of each passing moment – this
is why I love to spend each day with you.
We deal with unpredictable weather
but that is just a normal part of life.
We'll get through it all, you, me, together,
I am so fortunate that you're my wife.
I have just one request, sweetheart of mine:
O darling, will you be my Valentine?

Apollo's Revenge
2-14-21.iii

The Raven's talons clasped the golden bowl
    and flew with it to a fig tree.
Apollo had asked him watèr to bring,
    but the Raven got distracted.
He sat and waited 'til the figs were ripe –
    only then remembered his task!
Caught he a water-snake and brought it back
    and on it his delay he blamed.
Enraged Apollo's punishment was this,
    it may seem like a strange reward:
He set the Raven, Bowl, and Snake in stars,
    and on this night all three shall rise!

Lupercalia
2-15-21.iii

But 'tis the day for Love, O Lupercal,
when priests of Faunus through the thronged streets ran
recalling times when all of us ran wild,
before our modern culture and our ways,
before our money, houses, full-time jobs,
before depression, prisons, and our wars,
before our agriculture or herding,
before we had language, or even clothes:
'twas then that we were free, happy and wild,
and that's the time the goat-god represents;
'twas then we truly one another loved,
that's why we celebrate our day of Love!

The Romans told a tale of origin
explaining how Lupercalia began:
perhaps when founding Romulus one day
some cattle thieves chased off while he was naked;
perhaps tradition to evoke through time
of ritual in outdoor groves of trees
the goddess to invoke, goddess of love,
the love of home and fam'ly life and kids,
the soft Lucina aspect of Juno
whose voice rang from the sky, trees echoing
obscure pronouncement that sounded quite rude –
how could a he-goat go inside a woman?
The priest interprets this as metaphor,
the goat he butchers, cuts strips of its hide,
and with them whips the willing women, who
perhaps were so turned on they all went home
and fucked their husbands – well, what we do know
is that those women, in quite nine more months,
each had a baby. Thus tradition's born!

Susan B. Anthony's Birthday
2.15.21.iv

Beginning with her work 'gainst slavery
she was always to justice devoted,
and for her passion for equality
so many years later she is still noted.
She also joined campaigns 'gainst alcohol
with Elizabeth Cady Stanton her friend.
Their own group forced to create after all,
when for gender, speaking engagement was banned.
Through decades of speaking, she awareness raised
for the plight of women, who had no vote –
promote equality, her name be praised,
let all the children learn her tale by rote!
For few've helped change so much in history
as our hero, Susan B. Anthony.

President's Day (Observed)
Third Monday in February (2.15.21.v)

Today is President's Day Observed,
it's usually a bank holiday;
but with the ice storms, it's a bit absurd
to keep talking; what can I say?
    I sit and watch the fire burn
    some day I shall return
of Washington and Lincoln tales to convey.

Mardi Gras
2-16-21.ii

'Tis *februa*, the month to purify,
for cleaning both the spirit and the home,
perhaps with honor paid to god of death
prepares us for the Spring's arrival soon
when Earth will be reborn and life renewed.
As a tradition, it's cross-cultural;
the Chinese New Year includes cleaning, too!
The Christians did not start it, it's quite old:
likely derived from Rome's Etruscan roots,
more properly from those roots which both shared,
perhaps three thousand years ago, or more!
Tho changed by time, tradition's still alive,
the month of Lent tomorrow doth begin
when ev'ryone repents of all their sin
and abstains from the pleasures which us drive
(pretending there's a balance, or a score).
With confessions our souls are naked bared.
Before the fasting month, let's have a hoot!
We'll party Fat Tuesday, e'en if it's cold.
A last chance to do what we want to do
before the fast, we're feasting, one and all.
In New Orleans, folks like to run 'round nude
and trade their party beads for a lewd boon.
So blow that horn, and give it all your breath!
Tomorrow brings austerities. Alone
each one confronts oneself until we die.

Lent
2-17-21.ii

The ashes are a symbol of repentance,
of mourning and sorrow, of grief and shame.
The ancient tales have many instances
of sufferers and penitents who rub
grey ashes on their face and in their hair.
Now Lent begins, fasting and abstinence,
a perìòd of forty days and nights
when we reflect upon our sinfulness
and pray we shall improve, and be forgiv'n.
What need have we for God to forgive us?
Perhaps the thought brings comfort when men hate.
Myself, I do believe that all have sinned
and all must learn forgiveness to impart
with tolerance for one another's faults
based on the knowledge that we, too, have strayed.
Let not this day impart false haughtiness,
for ev'ryone has sinned. Thou shalt not judge
lest ye should be thyself to judgment hurled!

Nanny Goat Marsh
2-17-21.iii

The clouds burst open, and a great storm broke
over the swamp called the Nanny Goat Marsh.
What kind of "justice" could Romulus have
possibly been dispensing in that place?
Perhaps it's for the best he disappeared!
Most likely the Patricians had him killed
for interfering with their scheming plans –
but all the Romans bought the fishy tale,
that Proculus his apparition saw.

Fornax
2-17-21.iv

O Fornax, goddess of the oven hot,
on thee we rely, but rarely give thanks;
yet long ago, there was a time before
the oven was invented, and people
would roast their spelt-grains by the open fire.
This method was quite fraught with accidents,
and oftentimes the grains would be all burnt.
Sometimes flaming grains got out of control,
entire cottages burned down in the night.
The Oven normalized the temper'ture,
allowing us to bake our breads and cakes!

The Placards of Rites
2-17-21.v

Don't mock the common people at the square
who know not how to read placards of rites –
it matters not what district they're assigned,
nor when disdainful priest with haughty sneers
announces randomly a holy day:
if people want to worship, let them pray!

Feralia
2-20-21.iv

A small clay vessel was enough to bring
an offering of praise to the ancestors:
the purple velvet of violet petals
to sprinkle out upon the somber ground
along with a few grains of precious salt,
a little wheat to sprinkle with it, too,
a slice of dry bread softened in some wine
are all the ancient tradition required.

After a sample had been sprinkled out,
this offering upon the ground was set
before the ancient tombs so dark and cold
along with prayers and words of ritual,
thus was Feralia ritual observed.

But maiden girls were asked to stay at home,
this was no night to show the bloom of life;
and all the other temples were closed up,
the household icons set by for the night;
no fragrant incense on the altars smoked,
the hearths this night were left both cold and dark
while ghosts were said to walk upon the Earth
to sample all the off'rings left for them:
Feralia was the Roman Hallowe'en!

Karistia
2-22-21.ii

The Lares were protector twins of Rome,
revered with temples, praised on holy days
such as Karistia, Festival of Dear Ones
which on the Twenty-Second was observed,
the day after Feralia of the Dead,
just as All Souls Day follows Hallowe'en.

The fam'ly gods were given incense sweet
and offerings of savory fresh food
and wine oblations poured forth with a prayer.

A holy woman came the night before
to tell the lore and wisdom to the girls
who had been asked to stay home from Feralia.
The crone performed the Silent Goddess rites
and slid sweet incense sticks below the door.
She from a small fish chopped the head, and stitched
its mouth, then sealed it up with pitch, and poked
a needle made of bronze quite through its head,
then tossed the ritual object on the fire,
and sprinkled wine to consecrate the charm,
thus binding up the tongues of slanderers
who may have elsewise spoken poisoned words.
Then spells were cast, and threads were fixed with lead;
she seven dry black beans in her mouth placed,
then spat them out to rituàl complete.
Such were the sacred Silent Goddess rites.

The goddess was mother to Lares twins,
her name in Greek was Lala, for "No, no!"
Her silence was a punishment imposed
when she to nymph Juturna warning gave
that evil Zeus had planned a vile attack.

George Washington's Birthday
2-22-21.iv

When his ideals and country called to him,
he did not shirk: he stepped up and went forth,
and in that role he changed our histōry.

A wealthy man with plantation and slaves,
he served under the Brits in his first war
against the French and allied Native tribes
who hoped to drive the settlers from these shores
(tho it had been too late since e'er they came).
The British won that war, but at what cost?
To pay for it, they taxed the Colonies –
for after all, it was the Colonies
who, one might argue, benefited most.
Americans rebelled against that tax.

George Washington was asked to lead the troops
based on the reputation he had built
in politics, as well as his service.
He led those troops for 8 long years of war,
and used guerrilla tactics 'gainst the sieges
the British laid on Boston and New York.
It was a long shot, 'til the French joined in;
but in the end, the British sailed on home,
"To hell with Yankee Doodle and his cap!"

But time passed, and all was precarious.
The government its vet'rans could not pay
and Washington squatters could not evict.
So Washington backed government reforms,
and stood he for the role of President
the which he did attain for eight key years.
He set the tone for governing by law,
and at the end of his term, he stepped down
and thus a great example he did set
for power's transfer in a peaceful way.
For this we praise his memory today!

Terminus
2-23-21.iii

By custom, folks to markers tribute paid
which lands of good neighbors do separate –
a fitting friendly rite, reminding both
the bound'ry 'tween their lands to well respect.

As Terminus the god bound'ries were known,
old Terminus who helped prevent disputes –
as long as neighbors did the god respect
they'd stay on good terms, rank discord avoid.
Each neighbor brought a cake and garland crown
to grace the altar, shrine to Terminus.
One man would build a fire of bark and sticks,
and in an old clay pot his wife would bring
a glowing coal from hearth inside the house.
He'd light the fire and gently blow the flames,
then add some larger wood 'til fire grew bright.
A sacrifice of grain to flames was tossed,
three handfuls marked the holy ritual,
and wine libations poured out soon followed.
A ceremony short was quickly capped
when honey comb so sweet was shared around;
but neighbors good who loved a chance to feast
slaughtered a newborn lamb or suckling pig
and from this made a meal, neighbors to share,
and to the god of bound'ries gave their praise!

March

March's Namesake
3-1-21

It's war! The month of Mars doth celebrate
the conflict central to our human lives –
for we must stand our ground, not hesitate
goals to pursue, *take* that for which we strive.
The songbirds have returned, in trees they sing,
the clouds are fluffy in blue morning sky.
Although we know not what tomorrow brings
the sunny days encourage us to try.
This is the month of which folks long have said,
"Comes in like a lion, out like a lamb"
but I just want to control my own head
with thoughts focused on who I think I am.
I'll fight to my identity define,
and soldier on until I take what's mine!

Divine Parentage
3-4-21

It's common in mythology to claim
a famous hero's parentage divine –
for how could such a fact be ascertained?

For only after a very long time
had passed, were famous stories written down,
poetic license fleshing out the lines.

For in the early days of that small town
that we have come to know as mighty Rome
the story we all know would've earned a frown:

'bout how the Trojan prince set out from home,
escaping the bright flames of great Troy's fall
and o'er uncharted seas his crew did roam.

Yes, if they'd heard great Virgil's tales so tall,
those early Romans surely would have laughed
far back in time, when their town was still small.

For Virgil had employed the poet's craft
the lineàge of Rome to give uplift
by weaving tales of Cupid's barbèd shaft.

He blatantly invented the strange myth
(perhaps inspired by Atalanta brave)
of wolf-pup siblings Rome's founders reared with,

after their mother secret birth them gave
(for Vesta's priestess must remain virgin,
 in that respect was treated like a slave)

although she'd not committed any sin.
When Silvia her twin boys had conceived
there were no lustful thoughts she held within.

Because of warlike Mars she was aggrieved:
he secretly committed that cruel act,
and poets celebrate horrific deeds.

Surely this tale has no basis in fact –
divine conception's claimed for its impact!

Ampelos
3-5-21

Precaution we must all be sure to take
when out upon a branch we clamber far,
for easy 'tis to make a bad mistake,
then to the ground we tumble, and fall hard
just like Ampelos, youth of lovely locks.
A juicy grape his arm stretched forth to pluck
'til suddenly he slipped and tumbled off
the branch, and to his death fell, screaming "Fuck!"
God Bacchus libertine had loved him well
and heard the scream echo from hills afar
as from the elm tree bright Ampelos fell;
so grieving Bacchus placed him in the stars.
Now even when Arcas from night sky sets,
Ampelos shines, so we will not forget.

O Goddess Vesta
3-6-21

O goddess Vesta, upon thee we call,
thou guardian of sacred eternal flame.
The Greeks knew thee as Hestia of the hearth,
of home the center point, its very heart
whence light and heat, joy, and cooked meals proceed.
Upon thy hearth we burn the incense sweet
and bless thy name as thou hast blessed us all,
for 'tis thy warmth that us in union binds
and staveth off fierce fighting clash of arms
as is the wont of mighty warlike Mars
for whom this glorious month taketh its name –
that Mars who'd slaughter all of us with glee
so he could watch our blood flow on the ground.
But thou, sacred Vesta, do rain down shields,
or so the myths of myst'ry do proclaim;
for thou art a protectress filled with love

regarding ev'ry human as thy child –
although thou hast no consort, so they say;
thy private life is none of our concern.
No longer do we shame our nat'ral life
in this these enlightened times – 'cept when we do!
O goddess, please protect us from ourselves,
for 'tis no wonder we have foes without
when we keep breeding enemies within!

Bloody Sunday
3-7-21

Police are meant to keep the people safe,
that's what we all were taught when we were kids –
except that's only true if you are White,
you're not homeless, and you do not look weird.
For non-conformists and minorities,
police view your existence as a threat,
and threats must be eliminated, stat!

There was a demonstration on this day
in 1965, Selma A.L.,
to protest fatal violence by police
who'd shot a church deacon quite recently.
As the six hundred marchers crossed the bridge
police assaulted them with violent force:
the air was filled with tear gas and their screams,
as officers set to with billy clubs
and whipped the marchers with their cruel bullwhips.
The bullies did what bullies always do:
if you describe their actions, they'll do worse!
They think they should deserve impunity,
and punish those who speak out against them.
In Civil Rights hist'ry this day is known
as "Bloody Sunday." It's a day of shame
when free speech was suborned by police state.
The balance is still fragile to this day:
always, dissenters pay the highest cost.

Ariadne
3-8-21

Poor Ariadne, who had been wronged twice,
was more sensitive to the second slight –
tho surely she had ev'ry right to be,
who had been brought from Cnossos o'er the sea.
For after she had surely saved his life,
and he had promised she would be his wife,
asshole Theseus, remembered as hero,
on Naxos left her, and away did go –
while she was napping he gave her the slip
and sailed away with his crew in their ship.
She was distraught when she awoke alone,
abandoned on an island far from home.
But through her tears of shame at her disgrace
she looked up, and she saw a stranger's face.
She married her savior, Dionysos,
known to the Romans as the god Bacchus.
He went to far off India to campaign.
A long time passed 'fore he came home again
and when he did, she saw he'd been untrue
with one of the slaves in his retinue.
(By definition, slaves can't give consent...)
But Ariadne to her husband went
and said, "Darling, your actions make me said."
Said he, "I have no wish to make you feel bad!
  I'll tell you what: if you'll forgive my acts,
  I'll set you in the stars." Yes, them's the facts!
The Crown of Cnossos, glowing in the sky,
is Ariadne, after she did die.

Harriet Tubman Day
3-10-21

O bravery! The Underground Railroad
took courage, and a steadfastness of will
to plan, and to rescue those human beings
who had been trapped in Old South slavery.
O Harriet! May we be more like you,
and put ourselves out there, taking real risks
to make the world a better place today.

The Springtime Month
3-12-21

Time was, the year began with March – in Rome
the early calendar had a blank space
for those most cold and bleak of winter months;
those two which now begin our ev'ry year
were not worth marking out, so long ago!
But March! Although the Springtime's not begun
according to the Equinoctial date,
try telling that to birds nesting in trees,
try telling that to daffodils in bloom,
try telling that to Earth so vivid gren
try telling that to warm sun and blue skies.
We see the ducks a-swimming in the creek,
a silly woodpecker pecked on our house,
the ants are back to crawling through the walls,
the floodwaters recede, and joy returns.

O March! Our praise to thee, the springtime month,
a time of change when all the world's renewed,
and there is nothing more we need right now
so bless us with renewing change and joy
that we may be renewed, body and soul.
No wonder 'tis, when Romulus of myth
first calendar made, it began with March:
foundation of the year when all things change.

Romulus and Remus
3-13-21

The month of March was named for Mars
    the Roman god of war
who was to ancient Romans prime
    in days that went before.

The Romans told a story 'bout
    the founders of their town,
those twins born to a priestess who
    had taken celibate vown.

Descended from Aeneas (prince
    of Troy from whence he came)
twins Romulus and Remus were –
    at least, that's what they claim!
And 'tis from that same Romulus
    great Rome first took its name.

Abandoned in the forest dark
    with no milk or baby food
those twins were very fortunate
    by wolf to be rescued.
Then mama wolf took them to her den
    and raised them with her brood.

Then Romulus grown up became
    old Rome's founding first King
and that's why after years gone by
    his myth the poets sing.

The Third Month
3-14-21.ii

We've said the month of March was named for Mars
who worshiped by the ancient Romans was,
a symbol of their fierceness and ideals
which led to conquering the Western world.

The ancient Hebrews named this month Adar,
it was the twelfth month of their lunar year –
the calendar is coming to a close,
and next month the great cycle will renew!

In ancient Egypt, the name Phamenoth
was given to this month in hieroglyphs,
each symbol representing a phoneme:
the birds and eyes and squares were letters then!

In ancient Macedon of Greek culture
this month was named Dystros, so we are told –
perhaps to honor Dis, the god of death?
I know not, so I can but speculate.

The ancient Norse named this month Goi,
I have no clue to explain whoi.
Was the name solemn, or great joy?
Was Goi a god? A girl? A boy?

The Old English name was Hrethamonath,
a month named for a goddess, as is meet –
all praise the goddess as the Spring draws near!
Tho as in Rome, she was goddess of war.

Horse Race on the Campus
3-14-21.iii

There was a famous horse race on this day
in ancient Rome, along the Tiber's banks,
a place they called the Campus, green with grass.
This was the second horse race of the year,
the first would have been held two weeks before.
But if the Tiber overflowed its banks
from torrents of the runoff and the rain,
the race upon the hill would have been held,
a temple of Minerva close at hand.

In his *Amores*, Ovid sets the scene[1]
describing how he would pick up a girl
by getting in her space until she smiled
all seated in the stands, as chariòts
did race along a track, with wagers placed
and all the crowd with excitement enthused.
Although it's sleazy, it rings of the truth.

The Ides of March
3-15-21

Die, Caesar, die! Ignore soothsayer grim
and on the Senate floor show your bold face
that we might stab you in the back with blades
in full sight of our peers, yes, publicly!
Tho we may pay for this deed with our lives,
our lives are a small price to pay to save
the people's rule, democracy we love.
Yes, we reject the rule of tyrant kings
regardless of the title which they claim!

---

1 Ovid, *Amores*, III.2

So be ye dictator or Emperor,
or Kaiser, or "the People's Party Chair,"
or even if they call you "President" –
all claims to powèr based on cruel brute force
reject we from the bottom of our hearts
and we'll back up these words with bloody blades,
so say we all! And pledge we all our lives,
our property, and our sacred honor.

So, motherfucker, bleed thee on the floor,
thy life is forfeit, thou aspir'st too high;
and like the giants, by lightning struck down
to fall from cloud-high slopes of Olympus,
thy fate is sealed by thy arrogant plan.
O let that be a lesson for all time!

Kalends, Nones, and Ides

In ancient times, a minor priest would watch
the skies, to observe when the moon was new,
and when this came to pass he would call out,
announcing the advent of a new month,
so closely was the calendar aligned
with lunar cycles: thus was reckoned time.
The priest called out the first day of the month,
and then called out a regular countdown.
The Greek word for "I call" became the root
for our word "calendar," still used today –
'twas also of the word "kalends" the root:
this was, in times of old, the month's first day.

The Kalends was the first day of the month!
It seems so simple when you understand.
It is confusing quite Bēdē to read
who describes Christmas as "the 8th kalends
  of January," which makes little sense

until you realize, he's counting back:
the 8th kalends is 8 days from the 1st ...
including both the 1st and 25th.

The Romans held a Nones holiday
nine days before the Ides: a day of rest
when in to town for orders field hands came
and priest-kings told them what they ought to do.
The Nones were important to them then,
and formed a cornerstone of Roman life;
along with *nundinae*, the market-days,
which were held every eight days (as we count).
The day after each Nones, Ovid tells,
was a black day, ill-fated by the gods
in memory of military loss
when Rome felt abandoned by their god, Mars.

The Ides, simply the mid-point of each month,
are recollected to our culture best
by that prophetic soothsayer of old
who warned the dictator he should "beware
  the Ides of March!" The Bard's immortal words
recall to us that most courageous deed:
democracy struck back with bloody knife,
and on the Senate floor fell Caesar dead.
But at the time, the Ides were just the day
the Moon was full, and shone with her full face
illuminating land in dark of night,
halfway through lunar cycle of the month.

We have converted to a solar year,
no longer does the Moon mark out our months;
but still remember we ideas of old,
for culture from the past creates today's:
yes, we look back, forever and always.

The Goddess of the Year
3-15-21.iii

There was a springtime festival this day
in honor of the goddess of the Year;
for, since the year had *once* begun in March,
this was a good time to a party have!
Upon the grassy lawn couples drank wine,
reclined or stood, and sang popular songs
and to each other wished long and happy life!

St. Patrick's Day
3-17-21

Today's the day we all wear green
(but pinching people's really mean).
Before we all get too far gone,
let's try to catch a leprechaun!
The wind all goes out of my sails
whenever that old banshee wails.
Let's sing the merry songs again
and tell the tale of Chuchulain.
Nothing could be better than this,
a-dreaming of a selkie's kiss.
And if you're spending nights alone
just go and kiss the Blarney Stone.
A hornpipe reel and jig we dance,
don't let the faeries steal your pants!
So pass the Guinness, just one more
before we stumble out the door
on this great Irish holy day
to old St. Patrick sing our praise!

Bacchanalia
3-18-21

The feast day of St. Patrick in our times
was likewise to the Romans festive feast.
Yes, just as in times of antiquity,
the selfsame day hosts celebrations still.
In Roman times, 'twas Bacchus whom they praised:
the god of wine and wanton behavior.
The Romans as Liber also knew him,
from whence derives our word for "liberty."
He was a liber*tine* also, it's true,
but he cared not what others might have thought!

Tradition holds that Dionysos waged
campaigns that conquered Hindu Indià,
perhaps an indication that his tale
was brought by traders from much farther East
from lands of incense, lotus, and ganja,
the land of saris, sitars, and tablas,
where multitudes of divinities reign.

To celebrate the feast day of the god
the people liked to bake sweet honey cakes
and tell the tale of satyr Silenus,
who on his head so bald was stung by bees
when first he tried to take their honey comb,
until his face and hands he smeared with mud
just as Winnie-the-Pooh did, in his tale.

A priestess wise presided o'er the feast
with ivy crown and knife for sacrifice,
the thyrsus, staff of power, in her hand
entwined with ivy, symbol of green life.

The Liberalia festival was when
the youth of Rome were granted adulthood
when they had come of age – they got togas
and earned their freedom from their parents' house,

most likely a tradition dating back
to days before the city life became
a year-round institution for most folks –
back then, the games were only for Bacchus,
not shared with Ceres, as in latter days,
and likely were more civilized as well,
not marred by vi'lence on the part of fans,
the way the fans at modern soccer games
sometimes break out in riots and in fights.

Minerva
3-19-21

Of Wisdom's goddess holy day this was,
her festival for five days was observed.
A fitting time for festival this is:
in Springtime all the whole world is renewed,
and Nature's bounty freshens up our minds
allowing us to try to be more wise
just like the serene goddess, be she blessed,
accompanied always by her pet owl
who, in *The Titan's Clash*, was "Bubo" named,
I know not whether that was based on myths.

Our poet, Ovid, that transgressive bard,
informs us that the festival's first day
did celebrate the day of goddess' birth
and free of bloodshed was always maintained.
Not so the festival's other four days –
the swords were sharpened that more blood might flow,
for Roman citizens enjoyed blood sport
just like the online assholes of today.

There is great wisdom in the homely crafts
of spinning and of weaving at the loom.
The wisdom of the ages has informed
the workmanship of ev'ry craftsman's trade:
the leatherworker, dyer, stone mason;

the carpenter and crofter, smith and chef!
And even knowledge workers do rely
on wisdom as they practice subtle arts
of teaching, and of medicine, and law.
And don't forget painters, and writers, too!
We all to Wisdom's goddess praises owe.

Let's celebrate her as the Springtime dawns:
Minerva, or Athena to the Greeks,
thy praises we shall sing upon this day!

Ostara

3-20-21

The day and night are of an equal length
today – it is the day that Spring begins!
Ostara is the Vernal Equinox
and tho it rains, the sunshine's close at hand:
it spreads its warmth and joy across the land.
The flowers bloom! The yellow daffodils
with bells that open like a choir to sing
their praises to the glory of the sky
and give their thanks for ev'ry passing day,
this wond'rous chance to be alive on Earth
surrounded by the green of growing things
that sprout and grow with vibrance and with strength
as life returns to all the land in Spring.
So be like as the daffodils, and praise
this opportunity to be alive.
We give thanks to the Sun, and to the rain,
we bless the Moon and stars up in the sky,
we bless the flowers as they bloom and grow;
we wish that same prosperity and growth
will bless all of our lives throughout the year.

The Vernal Equinox
3-21-21

Upon the day when sun shone through the crack,
its beam illuminated symbols carved
into the stone by ancestors so wise:
that was the day the people knew the time
had come to plant their crops in time for Spring!

The Sinagua people long ago
observed the Vernal Equinox each year
with petroglyphs they carved upon the stone
in Sacred Mountain Basin, Arizona
well over a millennia ago.
The Water Clan's Sunwatcher monitored
the movement of the sunbeam o'er the face
of a vast sandstone bluff near Beaver Creek.
More than a thousand petroglyphs were carved
into the diff'rent faces of the rock,
and many tracked positions of the Sun.
They likely used a lunar calendar
with nameless months, just as in Rome of old.

The people practiced agriculture there,
and irrigated fields with dug canals
to grow their crops of cotton, corn, and beans,
as well as squash plants with broad spreading leaves.
They built cliff dwellings, some five stories tall,
a feat of architecture far advanced!
(Although that may have been later on.)
They built a court for sports played with a ball.
The ancients weren't so different from us.

The markings on the stone quite clearly show
alignment on the Vernal Equinox
when sunbeam shafts of light made a straight line
connecting symbols on the great rock face
to show the people Springtime had begun!

Education and Sharing Day
Four days before Passover

To nurture future greatness in our nation,
believe we in quality education!
This is Education and Sharing Day
on the 11th day of Nissan month,
four days before the Passover begins:
remember we Rebbe Mendel Schneerson
who gave of himself, and made such impact.

The Gleaming Horns of Bronze
3-23-21

Of Tubilustria I wrote before:
Minerva's festival days, this the fifth,
was used to polish up trumpets of war
that mighty Mars guided the battles with.
Let nothing interfere with sacred rites,
gaze on the gleaming bronze horns with your eyes.
To Mars they offer up a sacrifice;
Minerva asks, "Is war ever wise?"

The Sun conjoins with the sign of the Ram,[2]
he who had surrendered the Golden Fleece.
Tho Athamas was hardly e'en a man
when Ino tricked him with her cruel deceit –
regardless of the stepmother's abuse,
for sacrificing children, there is no excuse!

---

2 The constellation Aries

Robert Frost's Birthday
3-26-21

You were an icon, genius of your time.
Your era spanned great upheaval and change.
You wrote blank verse, but you're best known for rhyme;
your creativity had quite a range.
You wrote of horse-drawn cart in snowy woods,
you wrote of firewood chopped and stacked by hand.
Your allegories asked what makes us good,
your stories showed a deep love for the land.
You took the road less traveled – poetry –
and spoke of the destructive ice of hate.
Your wisdom and your pain inspire me,
your broad int'rests and learning make your work great.
From ev'ry word of your poetic lines
your love for land and Nature truly shines!

Passover Begins
3-27-21

If thou shouldst wish for Death's Angel to pass
and leave thy firstborn son alive 'til morn,
then mark thy door with blood from slaughtered lamb,
a sign of membership – thy house be spared.
Their eldest sons all other houses lose,
a grisly tale from distant prophet days
of how with Pharaoh Moses set his terms,
release of slaves from Egypt did demand!

The feast of Passover begins tonight
at sundown. Celebrate the ritual
with praises for togetherness, and song.
Traditions ancient shape identity,
and last as culture changes through the years
connecting us with ancestors and love,
this holy day after the Equinox.

Palm Sunday
3-28-21

Events like this are rare within one's life:
to be so wildly welcomed by the crowds
they line the avenues with fronds of palm
and cheer to watch you pass on down the street,
a borrowed burro serving as your mount.
It is a glory time, so savor it:
success like this presages certain fall,
as those with powèr turn envy on you
and they begin to plot your certain doom.

Recall how Jesus joined Jerusalem:
the throngs of crowds all welcomed his approach,
but just five days had passed when all that changed
and those same crowds all cheered his tortured death,
for popular opinion does not last:
both cheers and insults fade into the past.

Change, Concord, Safety, and Peace
3-30-21.ii

To Janus, god of transitions, we pray
as all the world through grand transitions doth go,
the changes in the public sphere and news,
and changes in the nat'ral world outside –
the birds are singing e'en unto the dusk,
the daffodils are in bloom, calves are born,
and rabbits brown through undergrowth do bounce,
a flash of white from cotton tail shines bright.

Sweet Concord, live forever, that we may
all live together in thy harmony –
shouldst thou e'er suffer, mayst thou soon pull through!

O Salus, god of Safety, stay with us,
for in Safety we find our peace of mind;
yes, Safety's why people all live in groups.

O Pax, we pray for Peace deep in our hearts,
we long for peace in households, and on Earth –
but not the "peace" enforced by might of arms
such as the "*Pax Romana*" days of old:
for that's a peace that we know cannot last
and surely will devolve to conflict new.
O may we find that peace for which we long,
the Peace that comes with understanding calm;
and may we live in Peace for all our days.

Luna
3-31-21

O great and glorious Moon
    you rule the night
and when you wax to full
    you shine so bright.

They say you tug the seas
    and raise the tides
which helped free from the Suez Canal
    the cargo ship *Ever Given* – it was stuck in wide!

To thee all lonely lovers look
    and raise their eyes:
"O Moon please bring me my love,"
    they sadly cry.

In Rome, thousands of years ago,
    on this very night
the people walked atop the Aventine Ridge
    for a sacred rite.

Luna the Moon they worshiped
    there in the open air,
with praises and glorious song,
    with love and care.

Cesar Chavez Day
3-31-21

Cesar Chavez, who labor organized:
remember him, ye people who are wise!

The Great Depression claimed his family's farm,
compelled to California, where they worked
as migrant laborers in the grape fields
just like in Steinbeck's novel, *The Grapes of Wrath*.

His country Cesar Chavez served when called
during the Second World War, although
his Naval unit was segregated.

Back home, a veteran, a husband, too,
a busy, hard-working family man,
he felt moved to become an activist
and use the system of democracy
to benefit the people. That's the point!
He helped get people registered to vote
and advocated for his policies.

Farm workers, left out of FLSA,
had no minimum wage protections,
nor had they lev'rage to demand a raise.

So Chavez traveled with Dolores Huerta
around the agricultural valleys
of Southern California, where they spoke
with workers, and urged them to unionize.
It was a labor of most fervent faith,
and from the family required sacrifice:
Cesar's wife Helen worked out in the fields
to pay the bills while he was working towards
the better future in which they both believed.

In 1965, a strike was called.
The farm workers made non-violent protest,
just as the workers once left Rome *en masse.*
Chavez drew public sympathy with his
bold headline-grabbing leadership: such as
a march that wound down farm roads all the way
from Delano to Sacramento, far
away, some three hundred and forty miles!
The workers held the line for five long years,
until at last the growers had to sign
agreements to pay better and listen.

"I am convinced," said Cesar Chavez, "that
    the truest act of courage... is
    to sacrifice ourselves for others in
    a totally non-violent struggle
    for justice." These are the highest ideals.

Transgender Day of Visibility
3-31-21

If tolerance we wish to preach,
we must extend the same to each
regardless of how they were born,
how they present, or how they're shorn.

April

April Fool's Day
4-1-21

Hey, I have some great news for you:
all your dreams are about to come true!
Here's all the money you will ever need,
so spend the rest of your life smoking weed!
You'll have a great house with a magnificent view,
and never have any work to do.
You'll never again obey any rules –
nah, just kidding. April Fools!

The Rites of Venus
4-1-21.iii

The statue of the goddess must be washed
 to show proper respect to her
and all the Roman women take baths too
 to feel like goddesses, as well.
Beneath green myrtle boughs they shelter take
 recalling myths of Aphros birth:
for Aphros, Aphrodite, Venus, she
 the goddess is of love and month.
As old as Titans, born of red sea-foam
 when Oranos to Kronos lost.
But Ovid places satyrs on the shore –
 who cares about chronology?
The rituals of Venus start the month
 with emphasis on nakedness.
Uncovered at the bath house, they all show
 themselves to one another there
and offer up the fragrant incense smoke
 to Virile Fortune, goddess love.
Then getting high on poppy juice in milk
 that's flavored with some honey sweet,
return they to their homes and husbands bold
 with hopes to virile fortune get!

Good Friday
The Friday before Easter

Only a few days after your entrance,
triumphant ride through Jerusalem's streets,
you were arrested for rabble rousing:
tried, convicted, and marched up that grim hill
accompanied by the jeers of the crowd,
the same who welcomed you just days before.
The iròn cruel they drove through hands and feet
as painfully they nailed you to the cross,
then set it upright and left you to die.
You for your mother cried, just like George Floyd.
Then with your dying breath you said a prayer
that to your tormentors forgiveness granted,
a wish for peace such as few would have thought
while in the midst of painful anguished death.

But did your death solve anything at all?
Did those who murdered you feel better then?
By acting on their cruel judgmental hate
did those self-righteous bastards closure find?
I think we all know well that they did not.
Those such as they just move on to the next
with no remorse, just permanent outrage –
they always are convinced that they are right,
and always seek out someone else to judge.

Your followers were forced to meaning find
when thus their hopes came to untimely end,
but your forgiveness showed them all the way
'til your forgiveness was granted to all.
Now highway billboards righteously proclaim
you chose to die, to forgive all our sins –
if true, a form of human sacrifice!
Although your message has been mangled now,
your painful death ensured your words lived on.
It's not a choice that anyone would make.
On balance, I hope it helped more than hurt.

The Setting of the Pleiades
4-2-21.iii

A small cluster of stars
they seem, when seen from afar.
Dispersing from the stellar cloud,
named after goddesses proud,
such as Sterope bright
who slept with Mars one night;
Alcyone and Celaeno above
who both with Neptune made sweet sweet love;
and Jupiter's lovers, who number three:
Maia, Electra, and Taygete;
and shy Merope who hides from us
because she's off with her husband, Sisyphus.
The Pleiades on this night set,
their wonder we shall ne'er forget.

Easter Sunday
The first Sunday after the first full moon after the Vernal Equinox

From Vernal Equinox to first full Moon
and thence to first Sunday that follows soon
is when the Easter holiday is found,
when colored eggs are hid upon the ground.
With baskets full we do not think it odd
to offer praise to Easter Bunny god
who leaves us candy that we love to eat.
An Easter ham is always such a treat!

On ancient holiday of fertility
we offer wishes for prosperity;
and tho the goddess Eostar is forgot
by most, her name still lives on in our thoughts
when we all celebrate this holy day,
although most use a diff'rent name to pray.

'Tis Jesus who's said after death to live,
and all of our mistakes he will forgive.
No need to believe in angels or elves -
we really must learn to forgive ourselves.

King Juba
4-6-21

Juba, Juba, Juba!
Beware the Sixth of April –
O King of Numidia,
this day was your downfall.
Did you wish upon a star?
I would your wish had been granted,
for if you'd defeated Caesàr
his poison seed would ne'er have been planted!
    If Caesar had died in the field,
       Rome's Republic would not to him yield:
democracy would not have been supplanted!

April's Namesake
4-8-21

O Aphros, Aphrodite, ye of love
the goddess praised, to whom we owe our thanks –
O Venus, wand'ring passion, burning fire
who doth our inner narratives inspire;
mother of Cupid, whose arrows do wound
with pain such as lends purpose to our lives –
to thee we dedicate this sunny month
as all the world revives in light of Spring!
'Tis thee we call upon to bless our souls
and fill our hearts with love, throughout each day,
a lasting love for one another here
who share with us this world and our brief time.

May all our days be filled with loving thoughts,
may all our nights be filled with loving acts,
may love shine from our hearts upon the world,
and may all the world be filled with songs of love!

The Fourth Month
4-9-21.ii

The name "April" is from "Aphros" derived,
an old Greek cognomen for Aphrodite,
of love the goddess – Aphros, apropos
for Springtime when the world is all in bloom.
Although the Romans as Venus knew her,
still love's goddess was honored with this month –
or so I have believed for many years,
and wrote this claim into *The Pagan's Rise*...
and Ovid, too, concurs! 'Tis Aphros month;
to Envy he attributes alternates.
But ven'rable Bēdē has other ideas!
Professor Faith Wallis in footnotes cites
the *Saturnalia* of Macrobius;
Isidore's *De Natura Rerum*
(a diff'rent work from that of Lucretius)
and Isidore's *Etymologies*;
and *Contra Faustum* by Saint Augustus:
as sources all, to back up Bēdē's claim
that April's name derives from "opening."
In Latin, *aperilem* is the word,
for travel opens to the sailor then,
when grey clouds part and open up the sky.
No mention of the flow'rs that open bright?
Perhaps these men had not romance, nor eyes!
We can but speculate which is correct –
despite all hist'ry's weight, I've made my choice!

This month, in Alexander's Macedon,
was giv'n the appellation, Xanthicos –
a story for that, surely there must be,

but at the moment, it's unknown to me.

The Hebrews ancient named this month Nisan,
it is the month of Passover Seder:
although the lunar date doth fluctuate,
as Bēdē notes, they always intersect.
This month of Nisan begins the whole year,
this holy month begins the calendar,
and with the rip'ning blossoms, starts anew.

In ancient Egypt where the Pharaohs ruled,
where linen shrouds wrapped mummies of the dead,
the solar calendar was logical,
a system as befits the architects
who o'er the desert sand raised pyramids.
This month they named Phamenoth, seventh month
of heiroglyphic calendar of old;
on our March 27ᵗʰ it began.

The Norse of old called this month Singlemont,
according to Snorri (Byock translates) –
but single what? The meaning is unclear.
Perhaps this was the first month of the year
(just as it was for Hebrew calendar)
and "single" really means 'twas the "first" month –
my speculation no foundation hath.

In Merrie Olde Englaunde, this month was called
Eostarmonath, a month for goddess named,
the same goddess of love whose name doth grace
the Christian holy day that we all know.
Why not name Christian days for goddesses?
Why, I myself think it's a grand idea!
We thank thee, Eostar, graceful with thy smile,
for thou art like unto the Greek Aphros,
a fitting goddess for a Springtime month!

Cerealia
4-11-21

The festival of Demeter began
in ancient Rome upon this blessèd day
in honor of the Springtime as it blooms –
the birds up in the trees all harmonize
as leaves unfurl, and from the ground seeds sprout.
The season 'tis of Demeter's great joy,
according to the myths, for the return
of kidnapped child, Persephone, who was
by sick old Hades taken, dragged below
and forced to stay with him, a life in Hell –
six pomegranate seeds then sealed her fate,
and Zeus decreed she must yearly return,
for in this world all "justice" is a lie.

While searching for her daughter, Demeter
had wandered wide throughout the withered world,
and rested on the rocks so desolate,
'til Celeus, returning from his work
and bearing on his back berries and brush
a meager meal and ev'ning fire to make,
did pass that point, nearby unto his path,
when his young daughter paused from herding goats,
and spoke to the stranger seated on the rocks.
To heal the household's son Ceres was moved.
She gather'd poppies for to help him sleep,
forgetfully herself tasting of them:
and thus she broke her lengthy wand'ring fast,
to honor which her worshippers begin
the festive rites on sight of ev'ning stars.
The goddess, using all her magic arts,
intended child to make immortal thus.
She covered him with hot coals in the fire,
until his mother screamed in fear, and snatched
the baby from the flames, and sealed his fate.

The Romans say that Demeter Ceres
first taught to humans how acorns to eat,
and also how good grains to grow in ground.
She taught them how to till the Terran fields
and sow the seeds in soil for sustenance.
A sacrifice of salt and spelt was made,
along with fragrant incense burned on hearths,
an invocation made to goddess dear
who unto all the people gives good grain.
The priest with robes tucked up must spare the ox,
its labor is required to till the Earth!
'Tis best to sacrifice a pig this night,
and on its porcine flesh to feast with joy –
so then, as now, an Easter ham was prized!

The Cerealià was a bright time,
O people, don your garbs of festive white!
Put off the dark colors of Februus,
for now his reign is ended, for a time.

The Victor
4-13-21.ii

In Rome, this was the Ides of April's month –
the day of the full Moon, when lunar months
determined all the dates of human lives.
It would have been just halfway through this month –
the moon was new at month's start, and it's end!

This was a day to celebrate big wins,
or pray to Victor, god of fortune bold:
we all could use a victory sometimes,
perhaps now more than ever, in these days
when virus shutdowns have so changed the world
and on each other people gross have turned.
Cast off your petty grievances! Instead,
we all must focus on the victor's prize,

whatever that may be from where we are.
(We're told a cognate "Victor" was for Jove,
 who won his battles wherever he'd rove.)

'Twas on this day the hall of Libertas
was dedicated, once upon a time:
coincidence most fitting, when we think,
for Liberty rewards the Victory –
we fight for freedom ev'ry day, don't stop!
The struggle must go on, it never ends,
so we must celebrate all our small wins,
to give us courage to fight 'til the end!

Mutina

4-14-21

O Mutina, ye mutineers,
what came to pass confirmed your fears.
O Mutina, ye mutineers,
your hopes were dashed and came to tears.
Octavian's troops to your town laid
a siege, you were in blood repaid
for daring to claim you were free:
the Romans squelched you righteously,
Octavian claimed the victory
and ended Rome's democracy.
Thus ended Rome's long civil war,
'twas freedom you'd been fighting for –
your city walls had held within
the last of those brave assassins
who'd murdered on the Senate floor
Julius who always wanted more.
But might does not mean we are right,
and crimes occur out in plain sight –
like when those Caesars broke the laws
and were rewarded with applause.
Mutina, may you take your rest:
for tho you lost, you were the best.

Numa's Dream
4-15-21.ii

Then sacrifice a pregnant cow, and give
    the fertile Earth a fertile gift,
for off'ring such sacrifice was said
    the fickle goddess to appease –
so Faunus told King Numa in a dream
    in ancient times of famine harsh
establishing a ritual this day
    which grew in fame throughout the years
until the times when Ovid penned his poems
    and *forde* sacrifice was made.
Attendant priests to butchers grim were turned,
    their tucked-up robes all soaked in blood
as with hand knives they slaughtered thirty cows
    and opened up the carcasses,
removed the fetus calves from bovine wombs,
    then reached into that squishy mess
and ripped from cavity abdominal
    the still-warm intestines of the dead cow
and threw them on the sacrificial flames –
    a nice convention which allowed
the priests to "sacrifice" the nasty guts
    and from the choice cuts make a feast!

Imperator
4-16-21.ii

Octavian was only twenty years old
when he was named Imperator of Rome
after defeating Mutina at last.
The Roman people found they much preferred
to hand their freedoms to a dictator
rather than suffer long protracted wars.
Let this a lesson be for those who say
they would pursue ideals at any cost.
There are some costs that none will gladly pay!
When war goes on too long, support is lost.

The Burning of the Foxes
4-19-21.ii

The games to honor grain goddess go on
with gambling on the gate-eager horses
and strange barbaric rituals, it seems
in which poor foxes were tortured to death.
The tale tells of a torment back in time,
when a young lad who was but twelve years old
once captured a fox near his fam'ly's farm,
enclosed it in dry bundled grass and hay,
lit the poor creature on fire, let it go,
and watched laughing as it ran to and fro
spreading flame to dry grain where'er it went.
It burned that whole year's crop, it burned the house;
and somehow all the people blamed the fox!
This tale they reenacted ev'ry year
at Cerealia horse race, on this day.
They captured foxes, and wrapped them in straw,
set them on fire, then watched them run around
as those poor creatures were burned up alive.
It was the public's cruelty on display.
'Twas not so long ago: we are the same.
The Romans showed us who we really are.

The Feast of Cybele
4-20-21.ii

The noise of the processions fills the streets
as eunuch priests pound drums on their parade.
They beat and bash the bronze so brazenly,
announcing 'tis the Feast of Cybele.
Tho Ovid seems to question verity
of ancient myths, he does not challenge them –
although he surely took some liberties
in versions he set down and we still read.

Regardless, he reminds of Rhea's woe
as Kronos cruel devoured all her kids,
until for Zeus she substituted stone.
Nymphs cared for him upon Mount Helicon.
O Muse of love, Erato, sing for us
the chants that still remind us of those days
when dancers clashed on helmets and on shields
to cover up the sound of infant squalls
until such time as Zeus could come of age
and challenge his cruel father for the throne.
The orgiastic dance of Cybele
is said to hearken back to that event.
As women with their wine do wink and dance,
their nubile rumps they wave, provocative,
and feel the lust of Springtime as it throbs
and fills us up with joy to be alive.
A shame that Rhea's priests must eunuchs be!
Barbaric is tradition some still hold
that those who serve the gods be celibate.
We must teach them the Tantra, let it take
the place of old repression that lives on –
from Vesta's virgin priestesses of old
and eunuch priests that Rhea did demand,
to Cath'lic priests who must abstain from sex...
As long as sex is stigmatized at all,
and shame attaches to carnal desire,
there will be some who cross all the wrong lines.
O sexuality, detach from shame,
that all may enjoy safety and consent!
Let's celebrate the way our bodies feel,
with one another share our true love real.

The Sinagua Calendar
4-21-21

The Sinagùa people, long ago,
the First Peoples who dwelt upon the plains
of what's now America's desert land,
inscribed upon the rock symbols to watch.
Upon this very day, the Sun aligned
with certain petroglyphs, and thus they knew
today began the planting of the corn –
one symbol even looks like a corn ear.
Another such event falls in one month.
The people staged the planting and harvest,
an early crop in now, most in a month,
perhaps continued through Summer Solstice.
O plant the seeds, ye peoples, and prepare
to irrigate your fields with loving hands
to bring about the crops of sustenance
that fills your hearts with gladness and with song.

The Rites of the Shepherds
4-21-21.iii

This day the Romans celebrate the shepherd's rites
with ashes from cow fetus sacrifice,
the beanstalks and burnt offerings in hand.
Then three times over candles they would leap
and sprinkle water from their laurel wands:
this is the origin of witchcraft tales!
...

Earth Day
April 22

We celebrate the Earth each year this day,
our Mother, homeland, ecosystem, world.
We advocate protection for the land,
the oceans, forests, wild lands, and the air,
the animals, the future, and ourselves.
For life on Earth depends on life on Earth,
and we are all, one to another, bound
by invisible, powerful systems:
systems we ourselves influence and change
by the way we live: our homes, businesses,
our farms, factories, and transportation,
all have impacts on the environment
which we can mitigate, if we but try.
So come together, peoples of the Earth
and celebrate the world that gives us life!
Let us devote ourselves to bringing change,
to mitigate destructive tendencies,
and solve the many challenges we face
with love for our planet, and each other.

Ramadan Karim
4-23-20

Today is the first day of Ramadan,
a holy day of the Islamic world
devoted to daily fasting and prayer.
The Muslims use a lunar calendar
to determine religious holidays,
so the season of Ramadan may change.

The year I lived in Egypt, by some chance
in early winter Ramadan occurred;
but this year (my sister notifies me
 with her thoughtful post on Facebook today)
in green of springtime Ramadan begins.
Enduring fasting as a social group
is shared experience that binds them all
(though low blood sugar can take a daily toll).
And when at *iftar* each day's fast is done,
and people are allowed to eat at last,
they celebrate together, it's such fun,
the family gathers to share harmony.

Forty years old was Prophet Muhammad
when his first revelation came to him.
The beginning of the Quran he wrote,
and thus began a new phase of his life,
the phase which would define him for all time.
This is the event commemorated
by Ramadan's annual observance
during the ninth month of the lunar year,
from crescent moon to the next crescent moon.

The ninth of the Islamic lunar months
is holy, in the world's largest religion;
a time to fast and pray observantly,
community brought closer by this trial.
At sundown of the night before begins
observance of the holy Ramadan:
just as the Jewish holidays begin
at sundown of the night preceding it;
just as the Roman feast of Cerealia
did follow fasting, for its devotees:
after the stars were sighted, feasts began.
For Muslims 'tis the Moon to watch in sky,
its crescent sighting by mullah announced,
the muezzin call reverberates across
the landscape, as the people all give praise
to Allah for the bounty of this life.

The Festival of Flora
4-28-20

The festival of Flora for six days
was time to celebrate the flow'rs of Spring,
in honor of a goddess by that name
who made the flowers bloom in ancient myths.
We learn from Ovid that her festival
began this day, on April 28th,
a fitting time of year for floral joy,
let us give thanks and praise for Springtime's gifts!

Walpurgisnacht
4-30-20

A new beginning April's last day is,
it opens up a doorway to next month.
Rather than close a door upon the last,
this day invites us to enjoy the next,
like Christmas Eve when children lie awake,
but set in Springtime. This is Beltane Eve,
Eastern European Walpurgisnacht.
The merry month of May will meet the morn,
the joyful verdant month of high repute,
much mentioned in the madrigals of old,
the month associated with heroes
like Robin Hood, who Sherwood Forest strolled,
and good King Arthur who with knights so bold
held feasts and jousting for the Whitsunday:
now Pentecost it's called, this year it falls
upon the last day of the month of May.
So greetings, merry May, we welcome you;
with open arms and joyful gaze we smile.
Great thanks we give to April as it ends
and brings us into May, like a good friend
who drives us to another friend's party;
a friend who, though most welcome, cannot stay.

May

Beltane
5-1-20

Beltane is the first day of Merry May
a festive celebration of seasons:
ancient traditions thousands of years old
for humble agricultural reasons
invoking fertility and fortune
with bonfires and oat cakes, dancing and song
we bedeck the Maypole and dance around,
anoint a bright May Queen with tresses long,
pay homage to a local holy well,
gather fresh flowers to make a bouquet;
we greet our neighbors, and spread joy and cheer;
decorate our houses with garlands gay.
So blessings upon this day, and our home,
good fortune to all the people we love.
May we spread good will with our rituals,
may blessings rain down on us from above!

The Fifth Month
5-1-20.ii

Previously I had learned that the month
of May was named for the goddess Maia:
the mother of Hermes in the Greek myths,
a daughter of Atlas, Pleiades nymph,
a nurturing spirit of the mountains.
Ovid offers this explanation last
in his etymology of May's name,
and first presents two other old stories,
in arguing goddesses' voices told.
First Polyhymnia tells him the tale
of Zeus defeating Hecatonkheires:
primal goddess "Majesty" assisted,
and our fifth month's name is from hers derived.

Next, in Urania's explanation,
the name of May derives from *maiores*,
those elders who enacted Rome's first laws.
Last in Ovid's telling, Calliope
relates the story of goddess Maia,
and so concludes with the most likely tale.

For his part, monk Bēdē records for us
that to the Gaels of old, this month was known
as "Thrimilchi," the month of milkings three
when dairy animals in plenty gave.

The scholarship Monk Bēdē brings to us
records the names of ancient Hebrew months.
The month of May to Iyyar corresponds:
the second month, as they figured their dates.

In ancient Egypt of the pyramids,
ninth month Pachons is the closest to this.
To ancient Greeks of Macedonia,
this month's named for Artemis, not Maia:
hence the name "Artemisios" was given
to this most pleasant of months for livin'.

Up North, to the Norse, where this month aligns,
names for it meant "cuckoo month" and "seed time,"
as we're told in the stories
written down by Snorri.

Flora's Festive Climax
5-2-20

The festival of Flora, Ovid says,
was sexy like a flower, full of fun,
with prostitutes performing in the games,
men and women wet their whistles with wine
while they watched the way the women on stage
made joy-gesting jokes suggestive of pokes

to honor the goddess of floral blooms.
May Second seems to have been the climax
of the games, with a goat-hunt on the next.

We hear not much of Flora any more;
the Romans honored her from door to door.
The wife of Zephyrus, that breezy wind,
she also unto Juno was a friend:
she offered her an herbal remedy
and promised it would boost fertility.
Fair Flora many-colored, such a charm
supplied to Juno, that she conceived Mars.

The floral festival's plebeian appeal
confirmed when roadway built upon the hill
and games to please the public both got funds
from haughty arrogant aristocrats
who'd grazed their cattle on the public lands,
now forced to pay a fine for public good!

Star Wars Day
5-4-20

It's "May the Fourth Be With You" Star Wars Day –
not a true holiday, just a bad pun;
and yet, helpful reminder anyway
to think about the cosmos, and have fun.
For in *Star Wars*, the concept of The Force
is surely based upon the Tao te Ching:
a field of energy that runs through us
and permeates our world and everything.
By modern physics this concept's borne out,
by quantum particles and matter dark,
though poorly understood these concepts are,
we're learning more each day, gluon and quark,
the interconnectedness of all things,
invisible connections through us flow:

a field of energy we cannot see.
Admit we humbly, there's much we do not know.
We take this opportunity to learn
each day to understand and grow we try
and find our place in this world as it turns,
connected we are to all that goes by.

Cinco de Mayo
May 5

We celebrate the right to be free.
Freedom is the only way to be!
This day was Mexico independent from Spain
whose old world monarchy was such a pain.
So spread the love with fireworks and tacos,
and we'll enjoy this life, *usted y yo*!

Lemures
5-9-20

The Ninth of May's important, Ovid tells,
a day when people observed ancient rites,
they'd go barefoot and purify themselves,
and over shoulder throw black beans at night.
Nine times, turning his face away he chants,
redemption he asks for with sacrifice
and does not check to see if beans he plants
(but if some sprout up later, that's still nice).
Once washed again, he bashes on some bronze
and demands all the evil spirits leave,
instructing them to get out now, at once,
he finally looks back, and so the spell doth weave!
Ovid offers an explanation dubious
as to why this day is called by some, "Lemures."

Mother's Day
The Second Sunday in May (5-10-20)

To our mothers each one of us owes life
and motherhood done well commitment takes,
affecting ev'ry moment of the day
and often interrupting sleep at night.
Mothers teach their children the rules of life,
unto new generations show the path,
often at great personal sacrifice:
career choices, free time, and money, too;
for once children have become part of life
they are the prime focus of ev'ry day
and for this reason it is only right
to have a holiday to celebrate
the contributions that our mothers make
and shower them with gratitude and thanks.
That is the reason we have Mother's Day:
in my country, second Sunday of May
(although dates vary by place 'round the world).
By Anna Jarvis it was begun here
to honor her own mother, great woman,
nurse, healer, and pacifist activist –
and people thought it was a good idea;
with celebrations since 1908
when on this day all mothers we revere;
although we note per Wikipedia
historical parallels for this day
dating back to ancient Romans and Greeks
whose festivals revered the goddesses,
the mothers of the gods and of the world:
Rhea, Cybele; *festus Hilaria*
with wine and dancing, mirth and merry song.
The goddess worship of those bygone days
to motherhood itself paid sacred dues,
as is right and just: praise mothers we must!

The Rising of the Pleiades
5-13-20.ii

Exiled Ovid, famous depressed poet,
notes that the constellation Pleiades
has fully risen by this day in May
signaling, in his view, summer begins!

The Argive Effigies
5-14-20

But what's this I learn from that great scholar,
outcast poet of the Augustan age?
It seems this was the time, in days gone by,
to throw the effigies of Argive men
off of the bridge, into the Tuscan sea
as an offering to Latin Saturn
who, it must be noted, is not Cronus.
But thank the gods, we are all glad to know
that Ovid, speaking with the river's voice,
informs us this custom commemorates
a crewmate of Aeneas as he died,
rather than some mass-murder nationwide.

The Festival of Mercury
5-15-20

For the 15th of May, Ovid describes
the festival of Hermes Mercury
whose temple dedicated this day was.
To honor the god of commerce this day,
the merchants burn incense and pray for wealth.
Some hie themselves unto a holy spring
to wash away their sins with sacred drops
blessèd water shaken from laurel branch
a ritual purification act
to wash away the sins of all their lies
and ask holy forgiveness from the gods
although, in Ovid's telling, this implies
no intent to reform or do better:
they express intent to deceive again!
Perhaps it's reasonable to suggest
that Ovid was something of a cynic
although we know it's also probable
that there is some truth in the scene described.

Shavout
7 Weeks after Passover (5-16-20)

The Festival of Weeks next celebrates
the day the Israelites received
the Ten Commandments, graven stone tablets,
symbols of codified morality.
O light the candles for this holy day,
the Torah study to focus the mind,
and feast upon the dairy delicacies,
for its wisdom is like milk and honey.

The Eruption of Mt. St. Helens
5-18-20

'Twas on this day in May of 1980
our lives were changed when Mt. St. Helens blew.
The deadly eruption on May 18th
blew the top off the mountain – it much changed
the local environment for grim years.

But I recall a secondary blast
that sent an ash cloud west over my house
a week later, on May 25th morn.
When I awoke, it was still dark outside,
which was unusual for this time of year;
I thought it was early, but later learned
the ash cloud had blotted out the sunlight.
And when I went downstairs it was to find
my parents storing water from the tap
because we had a reservoir uncapped.
The deadly ash so densely filled the air
we could not leave the house for quite some time
and when we did, we had to wear a mask.
The ash-fall blanketed the world around.
It thickly coated streets, houses, and cars;
there was a layer, any time we dug
into the dirt, in all my farming days.

Agonalia Sacrifice
5-21-20

A sharp knife in his hand, the attendant
stands over the sacrificial victim –
his robe, tucked up, is more sanitary.
He holds the knife up high and asks the gods,
"Do I go on?" But they always say, "Yes."
For once the ceremony has begun
what pow'r could stop and save the victim's life?

The Agonalia festival took place
in early January, and repeats
upon this day, the 21st of May,
we are informed by poet historian
in his catalog of calendar days.

Tubilustria
5-23-20

All hail Vulcan, god of the artisans!
Under the auspices of the craftsman,
the Romans consecrated war trumpets,
and polished for Mars the musical bronze,
keeping them ready for Rome to ride out.
The leaping priests danced through the streets all day
announcing sacred Tubilustria
consecrated with ewe lamb sacrifice –
a rite also observed in the third month.

Eid al-Fitr
May 23, 2020

Eid Mubarak – a joyous Eid!
The festival began with the sundown.
With this day's iftar comes Ramadan's end:
through holy month of fasting all endured,
and now all celebrate with a great feast!

Eid al-Fitr is a day of joy,
a day of celebration, and of prayer.
The tribulations of the month-long fast
come to an end, and people celebrate
with joy the accomplishment of their will
and their devotion to Allah. Wishing
you a joyful feast day! Eid Mubarak!

Memorial Day
The Last Monday in May (5-26-20)

Today we honor soldiers' memory
who fell serving the great Land of the Free.
When they were called, their duty they performed.
In doing so, they died, and they are mourned.

The soldiers fell to Nazis, communists,
mercenaries, dictators, terrorists;
fell fighting for land, or against slavery.
Expansive wars we no longer think good:
hindsight may let us judge in luxury
whether the test of time their cause has stood.

But no such luxury had they
when to the battle lines they were sent away.
With dignity and quiet grace,
we honor them. There is a place
for duty, fighting, and sacrifice.
The fallen paid the highest price.

Whitsunday
5-31-20.ii

The seventh Sunday after Easter is
the ancient holiday of Whitsunday.
Known by the modern name of Pentecost,
it long has been a holy Springtime feast.
It's prominent in tales of Arthur King
when all the Court would gather and tell tales
of errant knights, adventures, and strange quests,
of chivalry, and pointless duels, and lore.
Then at the Table Round they'd pledge their faith
to Arthur, and to one another's grace.
To Whitsuntide was lent the air of Spring
and Beltane celebrations from of old.

According to the Church, this was the day
when God's own Holy Spirit did descend
upon the Twelve Apostles, and inspire
them with desire to take their message forth
and speak in tongues, to tell it to the world.
They said to love thy neighbor as thyself;
unto our trespassers their sins forgive;
when we are slighted, turn the other cheek:
for all the world shall be gi'en to the meek.

June

June's Namesake
6-1-20

O Juno, goddess of fam'ly life blessed,
thy favors bring fortune to those with faith.
Though ancient myths focus on jealousy
(philand'ring Zeus thou chasest 'cross the Earth)
thy worshipers daily and practical
implored thee for stability, success.
The month named in thine honor is so bright
for weddings it is an auspicious time
when sunshine warms the Earth and fields are green,
symbolic fertile bounty of Nature;
abundant lushness we wish for in life.
Whether or not we are agrarian
we all pray for success, prosperity:
good fortune, smiling with felicity.
For those, goddess, we praise thee and thy month!

Gods Within
6-1-20.ii

To introduce his work on Juno's month
the exile poet speaks of gods within,
to inspiration divine laying claim:
such is his right; for, him to paraphrase,
within we each possess spirit divine
which lights us up with inspiration bright;
and this internal fire, the spark of soul
connects us to the greater universe.
The force within is part of that without:
our very particles join cosmic dance.

Ovid's defense is somewhat legalese;
insisting that, of all, he has the right
to lay claim to inspiration divine,

in his role as a bard, singing of gods
(admission of metaphorical gods –
 why else would he feel the need to protest?).
Then, in an interview, Hera Juno
herself explains how sixth month got its name:
she says it's named for her, obviously.
But then her daughter, Hebe Juventas,
relates to Ovid alternate hist'ries:
that "June" is for "Juventas," she insists,
noting that the earlier months plan war,
but it is the later months that wage it;
only she seems a bit confused, ha ha.
Sweet Concord offered them to reconcile,
attempting peace to make with some strange tale
about how June is named for some "joining"
through past political alliance made.

The Tulsa Race Massacre
6-1-20.v

An unhappy anniversary
attaches to this day in history.
Tho this event goes down in shame,
lest we forget, it had a name:
The Tulsa Race Massacre
targeted Black proprietors
living prosperous and free
in so-called "Black Wall Street."
Inflamed by some petty outrage
the mob built up its evil courage
and murdered without any pity
every Black person they could see.
We need to talk about that history,
this event from one and nineteen-twenty
and far too many others like it;
we mustn't let ourselves forget.

Carna
6-1-20.vi

O Carna, bless us, goddess of the hinge,
who opens up and closes down so much,
from doorways to treasures to prison cells;
whatever door swings on a hinge, it's yours;
as is the first of June, hinge of the year.

The Sixth Month
6-5-20

Great praises are due to Bēdē of old,
thinker and scholar, not merely monk:
he calculated the course of the Moon
through the chart of the year, our calendar.
A great historian of his era
(few wrote hist'ries in year 700)
he recorded and compared the month names
as used in classical antiquity
to those used in his own time, as in ours;
but he also helpfully makes a note
of the ancient names given to the months
by the Hebrews, Egyptians, Macedon,
and by Celtic ancestors, Old English.

Thus it is monk Bēdē who us informs
the ancient Hebrews named this month "Sivan,"
though he provides no context or meaning.

To understand how our months coincide
with the months of the ancient Egyptians
will require me to finally understand
what "*kalends*" and "*nones*" once signified.
Based on the notes of learnèd Faith Wallis
the month that corresponds to our own June
in the calendar of ancient Egypt
was named Payni, and it was their tenth month.

Monk Bēdē repeats the propaganda
promoted by historians of old
that credits to Romulus the month names
including May for "elders," June, "juniors;"
but Bēdē also mentions the theory
that our June derives from "*Iunonius.*"

Moving on, our scholarly monk informs
that the ancient Macedonian Greeks
had named their month of June, "Daisios."
I've been unable to discover why,
whether this refers to Dionysos,
or it's a kenning for some other god;
but it's unrelated to our "dais,"
of that much I can confidently say.

Finally, the most interesting fact:
the Old English name for the year's sixth month
is "Litha," a lovely little label,
which means in the ancient Gaelic tongue
"gentle," for this month's weather gentle is,
a favorable season on the sea
when the waters are calm, "navigable,"
and the time is auspicious for trading.
Litha was also the Old English name
for the Summer Solstice; and for July –
we'll come back to this in a later poem.

We thank you, monk Bēdē, for wisdom shared
and look forward to more contemplations
of facts and insights you imparted have.

June Weddings in Ancient Times
6-7-20

He mentions his daughter to make a point
on scheduling a wedding the right day.
In modern times folks just go rent the joint.
In ancient times they'd have to go away
and tell the couple it's not time to play
until the holy Ides of June have passed.
Yes, Ovid tells us, this is what they'd say:
that if you want a marriage that will last
wait for the Ides, people, don't try to go too fast!

Feast of the Fisherfolk
6-7-20.ii

The Seventh of June was a festival day
    for the fisherfolk of ancient Rome.
As for the tradition's history, Ovid does not say;
    explanation provides he none,
other than lobbing an obscure accusation
    against those who haul dripping lines,
alleging that when they sell fish at the market
    they leave their bronze hooks inside.

Vestalia
6-9-20.ii

In introducing Vesta's festival,
Ovid accuses the bards of lying
when they claim gods and goddesses appear.
'Twas his invocation of Hestia,
goddess who was by so many held dear.
She represented the fire of the hearth,
and the hearth was the heart of the home;
invoking the goddess whene'er they cooked,
her worshipers were never all alone.

When 40 years since Rome's founding had passed,
40 festivals shepherd goddess Pales;
home Rome had become to such an extent
Numa determined Vesta to invoke
with temple round to build and consecrate,
with woven wicker walls and roof of thatch,
which later generations domed in bronze
and rebuilt as a stately round temple
(perhaps after the wicker walls burned down),
attended by the virgin priestesses;
for just as Vesta symbol of flame is,
so also her priestesses bear no young.
Remarkably, from poet's description
men were not allowed inside the temple
nor were there statues of virgin goddess:
the focus was only the sacred flame.

Ovid is full of goddess lore this day.
Saturn, it seems, had two wives while in Rome:
Great Cybele, of revels the symbol,
known to us as "the mother of the gods;"
and "Plenty" personified, goddess Ops,
the Roman mother of the goddesses:

Juno, Ceres, and Vesta, she of flame.
No "Flat Earth" conspiracist is Ovid:
he describes the Earth as a rotating ball
(though prior to Copernicus, thus centered);
but what the astrolabe of Archimedes
has to do with the temple is unclear.

Hestia Vesta does not often star
in the tales of ancient mythology
though her worship was once quite important
and thus it is remarkable to see
a compilation all in her honor
set down by Ovid to commemorate
this day, sacred festival of Vesta,
the goddess who stands under her own force
just like the hearth fire for which she is praised.

iii.

Mothers tell their children to weave flowers
into wreaths and garlands, to decorate
the mill-stone that grinds the wheat for their food
and the donkey that provides the power.

v.

I love the story of how Vesta saved
besieged Rome from marauding Gaul army
when the women baked loaves from dust and flour
and tricked the invaders into thinking
that Rome's stores were plentiful even now,
by throwing bread at them. Pelted with rolls,
food raining down on warrior shields and helms
convinced them that the siege could not succeed.

Matralia
6-11-20

Real people are complex, and their stories;
the stories they make up are complex, too.
A complex figure is Ino of fame,
who coordinated the wives' effort
to toast the seeds and render them sterile
to make Athamas murder rival's child.
Ino, second wife of Athamas was,
best remembered as the evil step-mother
of Phrixos and Helle, who escaped her
riding on the back of a flying ram,
famed around the world for its golden fleece.

Perhaps an example of myth doubling:
tricked by Ino with an oracle's aid,
Athamas intended an act troubling.
His son to sacrifice he held the blade
'til on the golden ram escape son made.
But in another branching of the myth
Athamas with arrow his son has slain:
theme of infanticide to shock us with,
the father by visions driven insane.
Learchus: splitting of Phrixos, with different name?

The mother of Learchus Ino was,
distraught so at his death by husband's hand,
with baby Melicertes fled because
she'd rather escape to a distant land.
But madness gripped her too, she could not stand
survivor's guilt, and from a cliff she hurled
the helpless babe into the deadly sea,
who rescued was by nymphs from magic world:
Nereids naked, led by Panope.
Into a god transformed one day the child would be.

But against Ino Hera a grudge bore
for having fostered babe Dionysos
the son of Semele, to Zeus a whore
who he'd burned up for making teary fuss.
The gods are horrid; ever it were thus.
So Hera showed herself at Bacchan rite
and bitterly at Ino she did cuss,
against her all the women to incite
until manly Hercules rescued her that night.

By employing rationalization,
since three names share one cult, the myths tell why:
cliff-flung babe survived, and transformation!
Although it makes no sense, myths cannot lie.
Accretion and attribution complete
the story of why Ino will not die:
as goddess Matuta, knows no defeat;
as Leucothea she is known in Greece and Crete.

To Matuta a temple was this day
by Servius the King dedicated.
Forbidden was its doorway to all slaves.
From Rome we learn institutions hated,
as well as those rightly celebrated.
Festival Matralia, 11 June,
the goddess with cakes propitiated
and the mothers of Rome howl at the moon
praying that their children will not grow up too soon.

Loving Day
6-12-20.ii

Today is Loving Day, the Twelfth of June,
a landmark in fight for equality.
Though racist bigots always say, "Too soon!"
this court decision changed our history.
Judges admitted, "It's not up to me
  to tell others who they're allowed to wed –
  so strike those laws from all the books swiftly,
  or else you white folks go to jail instead!"[3]
It's better when we can change the law with no one dead –
although far too many have died;
I couldn't count them if I tried.
I do not wish them to forgotten be
as we all learn the best way to be free.

June's Gentle Breeze
6-16-20

The temp'rate month of June regarded was
as time auspicious for to travel far
in trading excursions across the seas
to distant ports, exotic source of wealth,
by Britons of old, who Litha it named
in honor of long days of fair weather.
In similar wise, the outlawed Ovid
on this day offers his optimism
that the morrow will bring a gentle breeze
and sailors should raise their sails in welcome.
No explanation does Ovid provide
as to why from astronomy he's branched,
instead of rehearsing the day's history,
now tries his hand at weather forecasting

---

3 Although this rhymes, it is not strictly true in a literal sense.

based on nothing but an ancient calendar –
and yet, it is a safe bet, nonetheless,
for as approaches the Summer Solstice,
the world is wrapped in splendid weather warm.

Juneteenth
6-19-20

In talk of America's Civil War
there's intellectual dishonesty
among those who explain what it was for:
when they say, "State's Rights," they mean, "Slavery."
Though we can argue back and forth all day
about the best way people should behave,
it seems only self-evident to say
no human being e'er should be a slave.
'Twas on this day in 1865
the final slaves in Texas were set free.
Let liberty for everyone alive
correct at last Founders' hypocrisy.
Thus, as "Juneteenth," people today do celebrate
and final end of slavery commemorate.

Much time had passed, two and a half long years
since Lincoln signed his famed Proclamation.
People suffered indignity and tears
'til news arrived of Emancipation
ending the greatest shame of our nation.
Remember it this day, do not forget,
give honor to Juneteenth celebration,
and on the calendar this day we'll set
reminder that those great wrongs have not been righted yet.

Pay reparations
boost equity
throughout the nation
give opportunity.

Litha
6-20-20

The Summer Solstice, the year's longest day;
also its evening, the year's shortest night:
our hemisphere closest to the sun's ray
in Earth's orbit, making the season bright.
So nourishing is season's warm sunlight
the happy plants drink it in as with thirst
and on this day the calendar we write
of solar summer, this day is the first!
Lasting until Autumn's Equinox is rehearsed.

The Solstice of the Summer, one of two
major solar extremes during the year:
these far points divide our calendar through;
the prime of eight Sabbats, guides far and near,
just as the stars are lights by which we steer.
Although the hours of sun each day decrease,
the energy is stored by atmosphere;
we soon will feel the hottest summer heat.
We look forward to it, and wish each other peace.

Litha, so important in times ancient
the entire month was named after the day
in honor of when folks a-traveling went
just listen to what Bēdē has to say;
his voice comes to us from far away:
The same name to the next month is given,
and also to month intercalary
through which lunar dating is forgiven:
inaccuracy resolved in time of heaven.

Litha was the ancient name
for Summer Solstice; and the name
of the month we call after Juno;
and for our month July, also.

Two months together
of summer weather:
and *another*, meanwhile,
when needed to reconcile
lunar calendar, align
the dates into time.
That's three months in all
that by one name they did call.
So it's hard to overstate
Litha's importance: it's very great.

Observance of the Solstice, 'cross cultures
was central to the year since ancient times
as noted in the Mayan calendars
and Sinagua hieroglyphic lines,
and other sun-watcher monuments, too:
wherever Pueblo peoples lived their lives,
observed the sun they, the entire year through.
Solstice was known to the ancient Chinese,
Egyptian pyramids to it aligned;
round Earth figured by Eratosthenes,
calculations only lately refined.
Join the Druids for a sacrifice at Stonehenge
when you celebrate the Summer Solstice with friends.

Father's Day
The Third Sunday in June (6-21-20)

Family my greatest blessing is
good fortune truly looks like this
with wife I'm raising two great kids
by Universe we have been kissed

The insects chirp and birds do sing
as into summer from the spring
the seasons turn, and with them we
stay open to the happy things

On these focus our intellect,
not on shit from the Internet,
or clouds, or stress, or squabbling kids,
just change the focus to forget.

The Constellation of the Healer
6-22-20.ii

The stars rise on the 21st of June
in the constellation of the healer
inspiring Ovid to tell his sad tale.
A boy, falsely accused of advances,
fell to his death on his way to exile.
Aesculapius the doctor was nearby.
Prepared he medicine with magic herbs;
with this, Hippolytus rescued from death,
rousing the ire of Hades and the Fates,
who their own pow'r and dominance assert:
demand the death of he who would defy
and with a shrug, Jupiter doth comply,
striking the doctor with twin thunderbolts:
for his good deed, receives reward of death.

The Second Punic War, Lost
6-23-20

Syphax and Hasdrubal both suffered loss
upon this day. The Second Punic War
decided in Rome's favor was by these.

This was the turning-point of Punic War,
when Hasdrubal knew he'd been overcome
and flung himself headlong into the fray
to die a brave if pointless soldier's death.

Four years later and across the broad sea,
in far Numidia decided was
the fate of Carthage when its allies lost
a battle fierce: Syphax was overcome
by Masinissa King, ally of Rome.

Remember, lovers, scholars, and fighters,
never to take for granted future hopes
but vigilant remain, and never cease
to advocate for what you know is right.

Chance
6-24-20

Goddess Chance, the other side of Fortune,
each day we ask for your blessed favor,
and meanwhile swift time slips into the past
taking with it our youth and early dreams
even as we find joy in the present.
So here's to the Now! Let's all raise a toast
just as the Romans once did on this day.
They gathered at the riverside temple,
and whooped it up in boats, into the night.
About their necks they wore garlands floral
and in their hands they held bottles of wine.
The outcome of our lives is set by Chance
as much as by the choices that we make:
so says Machiavelli in *The Prince*,
and his guidance is always insightful.

Orion Rises
6-25-20

Returning home drunk from Chance's temple
a reveler shouts at the starry sky,
"Orion! Your fly is open! Ha ha!"
(or something like that) Ovid imagines,
before mentioning as a passing note,
Orion's belt rises on the Solstice.

The Solstice! The holy Summer Solstice!
These dates make clear the need for our Leap Year:
the solar calendar of Ovid's poems
does not with our own precisely align.

The Feast Day of St. John the Baptist
6-25-20.ii

The Christian feast of the Baptist St. John,
another Pagan appropriation:
a prophet's birth observed on the Solstice,
just as Christmas was fixed in the winter.
No accident of date: intentional!
In order to supplant the traditions
of nature-worshiping locals, the priests
took Pagan holidays, made them their own:
directed society from without.
People still celebrate a Bonfire Night
in Celtic Ireland's green and rolling hills,
clearly tradition from the Pagan past.
Through social media a post I found,[4]
of other ceremonies it informs:

---

4 https://inews.co.uk/light-relief/offbeat/summer-solstice-2020-rituals-longest-day-of-the-year-meaning-stonehenge-shamans-celebrations-451208

an International Day of Yoga,
recent tradition for ancient practice;
the Feast of St. John, on various dates;
Mongolian shamanistic bonfires,
once outlawed, still important to culture;
Ivan Kupala Day in the Ukraine;
a merry "Maypole" dance in old Sweden;
and Finland remembers an ancient god
name Ukko. The Ukon Juhla bonfires
burn by the lake shore on Summer Solstice
in celebration of the longest day.

The Lares Twins
6-27-20.ii

The twin sons of Lara and Mercury
were twin protectors as the Lares known;
today the people left garlands of flowers
upon their sacred shrine in ancient times.
To Jupiter this day was sacred, too:
his temple was near Rome's Palatine gate,
founded by Romulus, as Ovid tells,
in Empire's mythical prehistory.

The Stonewall Riots
6-28-20

In a free country, it seems kind of odd
when we consider past events today,
the police had a Public Morals Squad
just to arrest people for being gay.
The cops themselves could not claim to be good:
they were taking bribes from the Mafia!
They treated detainees as no one should.
Groping and beating inspired hysteria
outside the Stonewall Inn late in the night.

A crowd gathered and police lost control.
For the first time, those gays put up a fight
and drove away fascist police patrol!
The riots that began that night have set the stage:
the fight for equality always takes courage.

The Riots of Stonewall let people say
that neither the gov'nor nor *pontifex*
should make it illegal just to be gay;
nobody's business with whom you have sex.
Perhaps it is not a coincidence
in a lower-class district this occurred.
With nothing left to lose, 'twas more intense:
they were tired of never saying a word.
The homeless youths, male prostitutes, gay guys,
butch lesbians, transvestites gathered there
rebelled against society's cruel lies,
when promised freedom disappeared in air.
A freedom for one must be freedom for us all.
Denying freedom for some is the way we fall.

The Last Day of June
6-30-20

June, you've been good to us; we give you thanks
and look forward to your return next year.

July, we bid you welcome, the morrow
dawns splendid in the sunlight of freedom.

July

July's Namesake
7-1-20

Hail Caesar, you who were stabbed in the back
by Senators who believed in freedom –
they martyred themselves to democracy
when public sentiment favored tyrants.
Even today, the seventh month is named
after you, Julius, voted a god
by those ass-kissing cowards, posturing,
always aligning for appearances.
Perhaps it would be better if this month
were still named Quintilis for its number
rather than remember a dictator
whose civil war began the slow decline
of Rome, from the mightiest Republic
to an overstretched Empire, mismanaged,
susceptible to attack there at home
while depraved lunatics claimed leadership.
July in summer, a beautiful month,
named after a cruel egomaniac
who never should have crossed the Rubicon
had he a single shred of decency,
loyalty, or respect for Roman law.
No, Julius cared only for himself,
and so we honor him up to this day
with a salad, a blended orange drink,
and an entire month, all named after him.

A Correction
7-1-20.ii

My wife compels me to correct myself:
the salad is not named for Julius.
The Caesar Salad is named for the chef
who invented it: his name was Cesar.
Perhaps I should write a poem just for him,
and another for the orange juice stand guy.

The Seventh Month
7-1-20.iii

Monk Bēdē, scholar from the Ages Dark,
your words enlighten us in these dark times.
Bēdē reminds us that to the Pagans
who made the ancient lunar calendar
of the pre-literate British Islands,
the seventh month, like the sixth, was Litha,
named after the all-important Solstice,
so central to their lives that in some years
an intercalary month was added
between Litha and Litha; named the same.

But Snorri Sturluson in *Prose Edda*
informs us that to the Northern peoples
the seventh month was known as the Sun Month;
it was the month of upcountry pastures.

The Macedonian Greeks (says Bēdē)
named this month Panemos, for the god Pan
(that's an assumption I am willing to make)
because these hot days of the summertime
evoke the wildness of the nature god.

The ancient Hebrews named this month Tammuz;
it was the fourth month of their calendar,
which was also aligned with the pale moon.

The ancient Egyptians loved precision
in their architecture and calendar
as well as in their military ranks.
A solar calendar they developed
to simplify "the reckoning of time."
The month most clearly aligning to this
was called Epieph, their eleventh month.

Bēdē does not indicate what this name
might have meant to the Egyptians of old –
perhaps further research will make it clear,
but I have no time for that rabbit hole,
there are bills to pay, and more.

Freedom and Equality
7-4-20

O Freedom and Equality, we call
upon thee to bless us. Thou art ideals
which we hold up in times of strife and stress.
Yes! There is something worth believing in,
although all the world is filled with despair.
Though threatened by dark times, deadly virus,
police brutality, and hopelessness,
still we find purpose, and carry onwards
when we think of our ideals: of Freedom,
Justice, Equality, Democracy;
and while we're at it, let's pray for Peace.

Independence Day
7.4.20.ii

We celebrate on the Fourth of July
to commemorate a specific event:
this was the day on which the Founders signed
the Declaration of Independence,
when the American colonials
flipped the figurative bird at the British
and said, "You can't boss us around no more!"
The war had started; now it was formal,
and would not end until rebellion was
crushed, or else the British gave up and left.

Quibbling Over Symbolism
7-4-20.iii

Nowadays there are people who quibble,
"Not everyone signed on the Fourth!" they say.
Can you imagine what they would have said
given the chance to argue 'bout each day
with Ovid, as he the Fasti prepared
and set down the holidays in his verse
despite all the time he'd taken to learn
in holiday lore himself to immerse.
A holiday like this is a symbol,
it's not always going to be quite exact.
Reasonable people will understand
the diff'rence between "symbol" and "a fact."

Let's Celebrate!
7-4-20.iv

As a symbol of freedom
let's celebrate the Fourth of July,
then go back to work on the morrow
exalting all our ideals high.
Until we have achieved perfection,
unceasing we always will try.

Eid al-Adha
7-31-20

The shepherd Abraham is properly
considered as the founder of the faith
for Christians, and Muslims, and Jews, and more.
This Abraham demonstrated his faith
with willingness to sacrifice his son:
young Isaac on the altar, Moriah's
mountainside prepared to witness atrocity,
when an angel sent a last-minute sheep.
Abraham sacrificed that ram instead,
and allowed his son to live: praises be!
It is a sick story, if you ask me.
That story began major religions.
Now on this day the Muslims celebrate
the Feast of the Sacrifice, which they call
Eid al-Adha. This festival was
taking place during Spring Break in '01
when our Mom came to Egypt to visit.
We toured from Aqaba Gulf to Luxor –
quite a trek, what a crazy adventure!
Everyone around sacrificed a sheep,
and donated bits of them to the poor,
and left nasty buckets full of guts and brains
on the street just outside their front doors.

August

Lunasa (Lammas)
8-1-20

O great Lugh, forgotten now, once the chief
in times gone past, shining king of Celtic gods:
this harvest day is named in thine honor.
On August First we celebrate the feast
known as Lughnasadh; also as Lammas.
If we listen to lore, it lets us learn
the name "Lammas" from Old English derives
from the words "Hlaeth mas" meaning "a half loaf"
so named for the festive breads baked that day
by our agrarian ancestors – yes, yours too,
perhaps – to celebrate the harvest's arrival.
One symbol may have been a sacrifice
giving something back to the gods, a gift
to thank them for the harvest and invoke
their blessing on the harvests to come soon.
The ancients made sacrifice a symbol
of what we would call "abundance mindset" –
the faith, belief, and certain knowledge
that the harvests to come through this season
will be abundant harvests bringing joy
preparing the mind for awesomeness,
preparing gardens, weeding to work well,
and filling the spirit with gratitude
that brings life joy, and makes one pleasant company.
On solar Wheel of the Year calendars,
Lammas is the Summer Cross-Quarter Day
in between the Summer Solstice, Litha,
and the Autumnal Equinox, Mabon.

Lammas blessings upon you, dear reader;
may you enjoy the bounteous gifts of Lugh.
May your sacrifice and your gifts come back
in blessings a thousand-fold upon you!

The Height of Summertime
8-2-20

The month of August: named for Augustus,
this is the very height of summertime,
when cloudless is the sky of blue above;
the days are so hot we hide in the shade;
the sunshine is bright, winter worlds away.
The heat is so intense, some leaves get parched and brown;
yet joy is so immense, this month wears the year's crown.

August's Namesake, In Brief
8-13-20

Ruthlessly he rose to power in Rome
repealing the Republic to replace
the government with an Imperial one,
himself at the head. And along the way
young Octavian was responsible
for the murder or exile of thousands,
so he could seize their wealth and quell dissent.
Rewarded for ruthlessness with riches,
he attained his goal. For goodness, go grieve!
Octavian was installed as Emp'ror
by the spineless sad sack scared Senators
who voted to honor him with titles
(such as his moniker, Augustus "wise")
and godhood – rather than run the real risk
of losing their own heads to his cruel ambition.
After him this sunny summer month's named.

The Eighth Month
8-7-20.ii

The people of England, in ancient times,
gave to this month the name of "Weodmonath,"
that is, "Weed Month" or Bēdē's "Month of Tares,"
where "tares" is an obsolete word for "weeds."
This is the sunny month of pulling weeds,
those uninvited garden guests robust
that tower over plantings and our crops
absorbing sun and nutrients themselves
while choking out the plants we grow for food!
Pull those bastards up by the roots, kill them!
Life is a competition to survive,
and winter stores will fail when weeds do thrive.

To the ancient Norse, this was harvest time:
their name for this month translates as "hay making."
A month to reap and dry fodder it was,
in the sunny fields, before the rain starts.

To ancient Hebrews, this was fifth month, "Av,"
and that's all the information I have.

To ancient Egyptians, twelfth month "Mesore"
this was; the end of their calendar year,
with intercalary days added in
as needed to correct for the sun's course.

The ancient Romans named it "Sextilis,"
before the perversion of Augustus:
for it was once the sixth month of the year,
when Roman calendars began with March.

The ancient Greeks of Macedonia
gave to this month the name of "Loios,"
there is no indication in Bēdē
if the name relates to Leo Lion
or if it means something else entirely.

My learning in ancient Greek is lacking.

Likewise my little list of the month names
fails to include some important cultures:
Chinese, Hindu, and Babylonian
as well as Mayan cultures 'cross the sea
all used advanced systems of calendars
although I know not what they might have been.

Women's Equality Day
8-26-20

The great shame of our nation's history,
the shame which we are still reckoning,
is failure of founding "equality,"
when only for White men did freedom ring.
Women we love, they are a part of us.
Like slaves and non-landowners, they'd no vote!
Instead, they were told not to make a fuss
and to obey the laws that the men wrote.
But such inequity, it could not last,
and suffragists called for a remedy.
'Twas just a century now in the past –
we are not talking ancient history:
America tried to improve its government
at last, and ratified the Nineteenth Amendment!

September

The Ninth Month
9-1-20.ii & 9-2-20

September's name from Latin *sept* derives,
because it used to be the seventh month,
back when the month of Mars was the year's first,
before July and August were disgraced
with authoritarian monikers.

This month was named "Elul" by the Hebrews
in holy lunar calendars of old.

On the ancient Egyptian calendar,
this month began the new year: 'twas named Thoth
after the god of learning and writing.
There could be no better way to begin
the year than with an invocation to
the spirit of knowledge and wisdom true.
Good move, ancient Egyptians, props to you!

September by the Macedonians
of old was given the name Gorpiaios,
though what that may mean is all Greek to me.

The Old English termed this "Halegmonath,"
the Holy Month, during which they performed
sacred rites to give thanks for the harvest
and to prepare themselves for the winter.

The Old Norse named this month "grain-reaping month,"
for it was the time to go to the fields
with sickle in hand, cut the golden grain,
sheave it, thresh it, store it away from mice.

From Internet postings I've also learned,
how the Old Norse marked out the passing year
on wooden staff rulers engraved with runes
and symbols, denoting the market days
and the days of special significance.
Their "Tvimånað" overlapped September,
beginning in what we now call August
continuing through the twentieth day
of what is now the ninth month of the year.
Presumably, the "Tvi" root word means "grain."
The symbol they engraved on the primstav
for the first day of our September month
a mill stone represented, or a branch
used to measure the water in the stream
which would power the heavy grinding wheel.
They prayed for rain, not for ice, on this day.

Quite strange it seems to think of ice today
while in the summer heat and bright sunlight
I gaze upon the parched and withered grass.
But shorter grow the days, darker the morns,
and summer soon shall end: all things must pass.

Gamle Barsok
9-5-20.iii

The primstav of the Norse was marked with dates
reminding folks they must care for their farms,
performing certain tasks before weather
would make them impossible to complete.
Cattle must return from summer pasture
by 'Gamle barsok' (our September 5th)
so they may be kept close through winter time –
else scary 'huldrefolk' might eat the cows!

Labor Day
The First Monday in September (9-7-20)

The benefits of capitalism
accrue to the owners at the apex
while the multitudes doing all the work
are treated as disposable objects.
The common people, called the "laborers,"
are required to work throughout their whole lives
for barely a pittance of remittance,
not even enough to pay a house rent
without taking two jobs, or else roommates –
never mind such extravagances as
health care, nutritious food, exercise time:
such luxuries are reserved for the rich!
On Labor Day we honor everyone
who devotes their life to society,
devoutly working day in and day out.
This day also reminds us of hard-won
workers' rights, that were not always thought so:
the forty hour work week, and overtime,
weekends, eight hour days, minimum wage, breaks!
safety standards, the end of child labor:
the people had to fight for all these things:
these rights, hard-won, not graciously granted
by robber baron monopoly trusts
or multinational conglomerates.
A corporation is a pile of cash,
it's not a person! It is immortal,
and its only purpose is to grow more,
to become a bigger and bigger pile,
maybe pay out shareholder dividends,
more often compensate executives
with ludicrous bonuses and huge perks.
A company's purpose is not to help
its workers; or its customers, really,
unless it has a socially-conscious

Board of Directors who all guide it thus.
Until the day when our system changes,
the working people must keep on fighting
to be treated with decency at work,
to be paid a wage that they can live on,
and to be recognized as essential:
truly every worker is essential,
that is the reason for their employment;
so let us give them all good praise and thanks!

September 11
9-11-20

It was 19 years ago on this day,
September 11, 2001,
extremist hijackers murdered thousands
using commercial airliners as bombs
to destroy the World Trade Center buildings
and the Pentagon, wanting to start shit,
a mad act of unprovoked aggression
which *they* thought was an act of just revenge.
Of course, *we* know nothing could justify
the deaths of so many innocents;
but an insular mindset can convince
a person that anything is the truth.

I'd been back from Egypt hardly two months
when this act of hatred shook the whole world,
and it saddened me to hear my fellow
countrymen depict a billion Muslims
as all being just exactly the same
as the terrorists who killed so many:
for I remembered meeting, talking to,
teaching, working with, even befriending
such kind, gentle, generous, warm people
who happened to follow Islamic faith.
It never is fair to generalize.

Such narratives led to 9/11;
and the post-9/11 narratives
led directly, although incorrectly,
to a devastating war in Iraq
that sapped our resources and left us less
a global Superpower than we had been;
and we may never get that greatness back,
for those same people nostalgic for it
don't understand: their actions brought us here.
But on that day, all this was yet to come.

The immediate tragedy was pain
that burned the heart, seared with those images
replayed over and again on TV
of the second airliner as it crashed
into the building's side, and exploded.
Sister and I had met our grandparents
for breakfast that morning. Instead we watched
the devastation on television
for hours, our hearts filled with horror and sadness.
I returned back to the barn, my abode,
and stood there in the tack room feeling sad.
There I listened to a Morcheeba song,
that brilliant British trip hop band;
and their song offered the only message
that made any sense to me at the time,
reminding me that love can stop our fear.

Our Lady's Day (Vår Fruesdag)
9-12-20.iii

The Norse primstav reminded folks of old,
that on the 8th (or 12th) sheep should be sheared
so they'd have time to grow some fleece again
before the hardest cold of winter came;
and so the family could weave in dark days.

Old Norse Autumn Begins
9-14-20.iii

All fences were taken down, and livestock
was moved inside by September 14th,
which they marked as the first day of Autumn
on that ancient primstav of the old Norse.
('Twas shy of our modern Fall Equinox,
 which we mark on the 21st). That day,
they gathered leaves as fodder for winter.
(Farther south, leaves have just begun to turn.)

Constitution Day
September 17

Our Constitution Day commemorates the day when
way way back in 1787
    the Constitutional Convention
    said they'd done enough second-guessin'
and voted they for the document's adoption!

Rosh Hashana Begins
9-18-20.ii

The Hebrew calendar's month of Elul
prescribes a period of reflection
as the year draws to a close, ram's horn blows,
and people perform prayers of penitence.
Then at month's end, so ends the year at last.
On the evening of the last month's last day,
the celebration of Rosh Hashana
begins, and continues through the next day.
Thus Rosh Hashana is the New Year's Day
of the Hebrew calendar. Celebrate
the transition, the change and renewal!
The festivities are marked by the horn
called a shofar: cut from a ram, cleaned out,
and sounded with resounding blasts all day
during the ritual ceremonies.
Tonight is the night Rosh Hashana starts,
perhaps the night when all begins anew.
Gathered together, people celebrate,
enjoying apples dipped in sweet honey,
symbolically wishing for a sweet New Year.
They bless the food, each other, and the year.
May you merit many pleasant, good years!

Rosh Hashana
9-19-20

Be the head that leads into the New Year!
The shofar horn to recall purpose blow
and focus intent on self-improvement.
Renew aspirations, be your best self,
remember goals and intents on this day
of Rosh Hashana. Blessings unto thee.

Mabon
9-22-20

Mabon, the son who was stolen away
from Modron the Mother in years long past
has lent his name to this Equinox day
reminding us he was rescued at last
by Arthur the King and his knights so bold
acting upon ogre's evil behest.
They sought near and far, in those days of old,
to fulfill magical mystical quest.
Recorded in Mabinogion, the tale
inspired writer Aidan Kelly to choose
lost, found Mabon's name, and it has prevailed
as the name most modern Pagans now use
when we call forth our Equinox blessings
and unto the Goddess our voices sing.

Yom Kippur
9-28-20

On Yom Kippur, atonement is the theme:
with fasting prayer, and rituals, placate God;
confess one's sins and acknowledge frailties,
and make such amends as one is able.
Expunge guilt, find wholeness within one's soul,
repair relationships with those around:
one's family, community, and colleagues,
like starting an AA 12-step program:
in order to move forward, first move back;
acknowledge mistakes, resolve to improve.
None of us is perfect: we make mistakes.
Believing in our heart we're forgiven
allows us to move on and be better.
Ultimately, we never can move on
until at last we can forgive ourselves.

Michaelmas
9-29-20

The primstaves of the ancient Norse would mark
this day as Michaelmas: the Archangel
to honor and to praise, as angels fight
their endless war against the fiends of Hell.
To celebrate it, folks had market day,
a festive atmosphere and social time
to mark the end of harvest and the change
of season, for snow was not far away,
and livestock was brought in under the roof.
They'd celebrate by baking Michael Cakes
and wish each other lightness of the soul,
lest death's judges should condemn heaviness.
'Twas time of year for settling accounts,
"to change employers, move, and pay off loans,"[5]
– like Rosh Hashana, similar idea:
the old year is now coming to a close,
making this time to settle one's accounts.
Perhaps this hearkens back to herding tribes
and culture that predates agriculture
that marked this time as the end of the year
before the invention of the modern
calendar, with its New Year near Solstice.
I'm speculating now, but one thing's sure:
the ancients counted this a holy time.

---

5 Sarah Kirton. (n.d., c. 2002) *Primstav – an ancient calendar form – The Fall Months*. Retrieved from
https://norcalspelmanslag.org/ncsnlf2002/ncsnlf2002b.html

October

Stormfall
10-1-20

The air turns chilly in October's month,
thus the ancients named it "Winterfilleth,"
the month when colder weather falls on us
and our thoughts turn to morbid death and fear.
In *Rise of the Pagans*, I once proposed
the name "Stormfall" as this month's modern name,
but second-guessed myself and used "Harvest"
in my final proposal for Pagan month names.
I'd been too long separated from farms,
forgetting that the harvest is long done
(for the most part) by pumpkin-patch season,
even though corn mazes are still standing.

The Tenth Month
10-1-20.ii

Our name for October comes from Latin.
It was simply the eighth month of the year
when, according to myth, Romulus wrote down
the months, making the Roman calendar.
Later calendars moved year's beginning
two months earlier, to January:
the basis for our modern calendar.
That's how "October" became the tenth month,
identified by a misleading name:
how strange that the tenth month is named the eighth!

The Old English name was more descriptive.
Winterfylleth's a name with character;
perhaps suited to a colder climate,
yet 'twas evocative and meaningful.

The Old Norse "Harvest Month," offset two weeks
from our reckoning, ends mid-October.
Then begins "Gormånað," the month of gore
(just like the "Blodmonath" of Old English),
translated as "culling month" in Snorri:
the month when herds were thinned, and larders stocked.

In Macedonia of old, this month's name
was Hyperberetaios – likely named
for Hyperborea, mythical land
of endless sunshine, harps, and singing,
where lived a race of giants, beyond the wind.

The ancient Hebrews called this month Tishri.
It was their New Year: a new beginning
following the festival of Rosh Hashanah,
when starting over is a part of life.

The Pyramid builders of ancient Egypt
numbered this month the second of the year.
Their name for it was "Phaophi," Bēdē tells,
though what that signifies is not quite clear.

Sukkot
Five Days After Yom Kippur

The Feast of Tabernacles, Feast of Booths,
a harvest festival of grains and fruits
recalling how those huts so primitive
did shelter to the wand'ring peoples give.
Symbolic huts ye build now, celebrate,
give gratitude and thanks for seven days!

Oktoberfest
The First Sunday in October

We were all sad we did miss out
on a good chance to dance about
to eat some kilbasa, drink good beer,
and wish each other Bavarian cheer!
Corona Virus spun our lives around
with social distancing and lockdowns.

In Mt. Angel I've heard a polka band
playing "The Chicken Dance" something grand
while all the people danced with glee
and flapped their wings to the melody.

They had a party for Prince Ludwig's wedding,
in Bavaria, back in 1810;
and it was so much fun that the next year
they all agreed to keep the new tradition!

Cabbage Day
10-7-20.ii

On the Old Norse "primstave" calendars
    October 7 was Cabbage Day:
the time of year when brassicas
    should all be stored away.
They called the day Kåldagen,
    and also Britemesse
after a nun, named for the goddess
    of Imbolc's holiness.
Some years (folks say) there are a few days
    of warmer weather
at this time, when bears dig dens,
    and line them with heather.

Columbus Day
The Second Monday of October

Columbus changed our history,
now he now has lots of enemies.
So on his day today
I'm simply going to say,
"He crossed that blue in '92
  and that's why we're here, me and you!
  I don't know what we're going to do.
  Let's try to share the love and prove
  that everyone matters and we're all the same
  no matter your stature, no matter your name.
Indigenous and immigrant
all living on this continent
to one another respect give,
  and live the best life we can live."

Dinesmesse
10-9-20.iii

The day we know as October 9
    the Norse called "Dinesmesse" –
with bishop's staff and fish they marked
    how Dennis died in distress-a.

Norse Winter's Eve (Vinternatt) and New Year (Vettradagen)
10-14-20.ii

On our October the 14th
    the Norse marked Vinternatt.
The old year was all over now,
    the New Year was begot.

The Old Norse marked their New Year's Day
    on the primstav with a mitten.
By this time winter had set in –
    by cold you might be bitten!

Perhaps it's 'cause it snowed so hard,
    or perhaps due to the darkening days
they attached sleigh bells to their horses 'bout now
    to warn folks, "Get out of the way!"

The Pagan folk of ancient times
    observed their Vettradagen
with rituals, cleaning, and sacrifice
    to bring good fortune joggin'!

The Feast Day of St. Luke (Lukosmesse)
10-18-20.ii

The Norse of old to slaughter led the ox
upon this day, the Mass of strange St. Luke –
perhaps the wingèd oxen art explains
the association; or perhaps not.
The heavy rains fall at this time of year,
inviting Noah stories to be told –
this is a deadline for the harvest fields
when all the vegetables and root crops should
have been brought in and stored before this day –
or else those things will just rot in the ground!

St. Ursula's Day (Ursulamesse)
10-21-20

The Mass of Ursula was Maiden's Day
observed by the Norse to commemorate
the tragic slaughter of the pilgrim nuns
who by the Huns were killed outside Cologne –
in revenge for which the Huns, in turn, died.
A misunderstanding gave rise to myth:
an abbreviation was mistaken
for a Roman numeral, inflating
the number of the tragic martyred nuns
from eleven to eleven thousand.
That makes a better story anyway.
On this day, the boats were berthed for winter
before the seas grew stormy and froze o'er.
Spinning wheels and millstones were avoided
for reasons that are still obscure to me.

The Two Apostles' Mass[6]
10-28-20

On this day two martyrs old,
        patrons of those who've failed,
the primstav of the ancient Norse
        marked with a threshing flail.

Farmers should plan livestock to feed
        stored fodder, leaves or hay,
rather than put them in the fields
        frozen after this day.

---

6 Simon the Apostle was patron saint of woodcutters, which is extremely
gruesome because he was martyred by being sawed in half; and St. Jude (Judas
Thaddeus) is the patron saint of lost causes. Hallelujah!

So cold the weather grew up North
    that they could always know
they could travel by sleigh each and every day
    after now – there was always snow!

Halloween
10-31-20.ii

The ancient Celts called this day Sowan,[7]
the day to celebrate the Harvest's end.
On the year's wheel, it's the Cross-Quarter Day
and the Winter Solstice feast of dark days.

Celebrate the Dark

It is no myst'ry why this time of year
has long been associated with fear:
for all around the plants wither in death,
and in the Northern climes you see your breath.
All 'round the land is rotting in decay,
the dampness, rain, and mold fill each wet day.
The spiders build their webs across the path,
then end up in our face, we scream with wrath.
Our houses invaded by mice and rats,
in evening we are dive-bombed by the bats.
So nat'rally our thoughts turn to the grave,
its terrors from which none are truly saved.
Instead we learn to celebrate the dark:
dress up, get festive, and give life some spark!

---

7   In Gaelic it's spelled "Samhain."

November

All Soul's Day (Dia de los Muertos)
11-1-20

Between the worlds the borders open are,
allowing dead spirits to cross back o'er
for this time is the border of the year
when winter takes its hold upon the land.
We celebrate the Ancestors this day,
on Dia de los Muertos, as it's called,
or All Soul's Day, the name I learned in school;
which lends its name to last night's festival:
All Hallow's Eve contraction, Halloween.
The pumpkins are a symbol of Harvest,
but Jack-o-Lanterns were in old times carved
from turnips, and other sturdy foodstuffs
to ward off scary creatures of the night.
We celebrate our fears and our ancestors,
we celebrate family togetherness;
we celebrate stomachs full of candy!

Election Day
11-3-20
(The first Tuesday in November, once every 4 years)

We've waited for this day for four long years.
The outcome will bring either joy or tears.
We hope things will begin to go our way:
we hope to see a landslide win today!

Guy Fawkes Day
11-5-20.iii

Guy Fawkes Day already has its own poem;
thanks to "V for Vendetta," its words are well-known.
Despite the gunpowder treason and plot,
the 5th of November I have forgot!

It seems an odd thing, folks would celebrate
the near-death of all those who legislate –
bespeaks uneasy truce with what we list.
Guy Fawkes was totally a terrorist
who placed gunpowder beneath Parliament
so those leaders would all to Hell be sent.
I hope we can agree, ladies and gents,
that *killing* should not decide the government.

The Eleventh Month
11-5-20.ii

November, month named after a number
that's no longer the number of the month!
When Rome was young, the month of Mars began
the calendar, before all went astray.
Were two months added? Were two months renamed?
Although both of these statements may be true,
this is still not the ninth month of the year.
Other ancient peoples had better names.

For November, the ancient Hebrew name
(or the lunar month that's closest to it)
serene "Marheshvan," a name exotic.

To the Egyptians of cat sacrifice,
this was the month of Hathyr. It was named
for Hathor, I would guess: the new goddess
who nursed the Pharaohs, like Queen Hatshepsut.

In Macedonia, which shared Greek culture,
this was the month which people named Dios.
The meaning of this month seems obvious:
this was a holy month, thanks be to gods!

A holy month this was to Old English,
though with a different commemoration:
this was the gory month of Blodmonath,
when blood was spilled, and livestock stocked larders.
This was the month to cull from out the herd
such animals as would not last winter
and put them on the table for to feast,
all the while giving thanks unto the gods.

The ancient Norse month name is quite the same
(and likely lined up along the same dates) –
the Norse called this month Gormonað,
the month of gore, when blood was spilled on farms,
the same tradition as the British Isles
and likely 'cross the ancient Gaelic world.

Bear Evening (Bjørnekvelden)
11-11-20

The primstav of the Norse declares today
the day from which the whole month took its name
when animals were to the slaughter led
and then dispatched by hand, 'midst blood and gore.
The people had a closer connection
to the source of their sustenance back then
when in their fields they grew their vegetables
and slaughtered livestock with their very hands,

the blood a-gushing out upon the floor
as in their death throes creatures thrashed about
and then lay still at last, to breathe no more.
They'd slit from stem to stern, and then pull out
the guts still warm, the squishy slimy gore.
We're far removed from this reality
in these days when we buy meat from the store!

If he's a man with honor to his name,
the miller would not grind the grain this day;
perhaps out of respect for the livestock,
or promise not to cut grain with bone meal?
The connection is unclear in my source.

It is clear that winter was setting in:
this is the day when bears went to their dens;
and hungry winter storms would strike the land
gnashing their teeth and howling through the night!

Veteran's Day
11-11-20.ii

Today's the day we praise our veterans
    who fought in this great nation's many wars.
These brave folks did the best they could have done
    in battles lost and battles won.

Diwali
11-14-20.ii

Diwali is the festival of lights
that's celebrated widely by Hindus
when fireworks and candles brighten the night
and people feast, as people like to do!
This grand holy festival lasts five days
to honor Lakshmi, of prosperity
the goddess, who brings all good things and stays
throughout the Fall harvest festivities!
It's Halloween and Thanksgiving combined
in terms of its cultural importance.
It put folks in a grateful state of mind
and gives them a reason to have a dance!
No moonlight – it's the darkest night of the year,
so celebrations drive away all fear!

Mary's Day
11-21-20

The practice of community storage
of certain essential items of worth
surely predates historical accounts.
The temple of Ceres, in Roman times,
was used to store the laws, and seed for crops.
Likewise, the ancient Norse in churches stored
necessities to see them through hard times.
This was the day the primstav marked to go
unto the church, to donate wool and cloth.
The church in turn for fun would parcel out
to pretty women young throughout the town
some garters for their stockings ("hosebands" called) –
a nominal token of "Mary's Day"
on much older tradition doubtless based.

St. Clement's Mass (*Klementsmesse*)
11-23-20

According to the primstav of the Norse
the children should not get much food today:
"Let's keep them hungry, so they will enjoy
   the feasting of the coming Yule season,"
apparently is the ancient logic.

This is a season of hard winter storms,
and frosts that kill green plants and eat fingers,
for those who live in those far northern climes,
thank the gods that my ancestors moved down south
so I could reside in a temp'rate zone.
The primstav marked a feast day on this date:
a Roman exile, just like friend Ovid,
but harsher still. Clement was sent up north
from Rome to a work camp in Crimea
as a cruel punishment for some offense.
To get revenge, Clement and some new friends
destroyed the temples of the Pagan faiths,
because the Romans were still Pagan then,
and in their stead built churches to his God,
a rebellious act with lasting effect:
to conquer a society slowly,
change what they learn, and what they think about.
The Emperor of Rome was Trajan then,
and when he learned about Clement's mischief,
ordered his summary execution.
So Clement was bound to a ship's anchor
and tossed into the ocean, where he drowned.
For this distinction, he is remembered
by a symbol drawn in an anchor's shape,
perverse remembrance of his grim death,
just as Jesus got the sign of the cross.
An aside to my loved ones who read this:
if I should die shot by some MAGA loon,
please don't memorialize my gruesome death
by drawing little gun signs everywhere!

The First Thanksgiving
11-25-20

We're raised learning the American myth
of the world's very first Thanksgiving Day
after indigenous Americans
had taught the Pilgrims how to plant maize
and saved the colonists from starvation.
In those days, both parties desired friendship;
they had no idea of the wars to come
later, when more colonists crossed the sea.
The rivers were yet so full of salmon
the settlers could scoop them out with pitchforks
and plant them as fertilizer for corn.
To celebrate the abundant harvest,
cross-cultural celebration they held:
Pilgrims and Native Americans both
sat down to table together as friends,
to show their gratitude and live in peace.
If only the spirit of Thanksgiving
had lasted, and permeated culture
as America grew and spread outwards
perhaps we would still live in harmony
with the land, its people, and each other.

Thanksgiving Day
The Fourth Thursday in November (11-26-20)

Let's fill our minds with gratitude
    and on this day give thanks!
We'll have a joyful attitude
    and stroll the river banks.

We'll feast and join in gratitude,
    bake pie, and roast turkey –
we'll focus mental attitude
    on life, love, and liberty.

It's a season of gratitude,
    and thoughts of charity
as we adjust our attitude,
    think as community.

St. Andrew's Day (Andreasmesse)
11-30-20

The primstav marks off Christian holidays
like today, the feast day of St. Andrew,
the patron of the fishermen at sea,
namesake of my once University.

This was the day the Norse caught their Yule fish –
a bit alarming, as it's three weeks yet!
The weather was so cold, the fish stayed fresh...
(or else they tossed it in barrels of lye
 to make Lutefisk, vile, nasty, horrid,
 gross, slimy, foul, disgusting Lutefisk
 such as we ate at family holidays
 when I was young, but never want again!)

My Grandfather's family hails from Beiarn,
I know because we're listed in a book;
and in Beiarn they gave this day a name:
it was Jul-Anders Dag, sort of "Yule Eve,"
the day before the month of Yule begins.
The people put on their fanciest clothes
and showed up at other people's houses
at dinner-time: a sort of Wassailing.
They would pretend to be from over hill,
and the hosts would serve them sheep's heads and feet,
which was considered no delicacy!
(A delicacy? Perhaps an insult!)
If visitors objected to the fare,
the hosts were ready with a mocking poem
which they'd recite, to make fun of the guests
for having such a delicate palate!

This also was the day to set aside
the wood which men would sit around and carve
on long cold winter nights beside the fire.
They'd let it season for a complete year –
wood set aside today was next year's stock.

December

Time Outside of Time
12-1-20

The Romans did not mark the winter months
in the first version of their calendar.
They simply began their year with our March:
a year of ten months, through our December.
The winter months before the Spring were blank –
an empty time of waiting for the Sun,
a cold time outside of time, a nothing.
But after while, they knew this could not last.

Two added months filled in the calendar:
new months, at the beginning of the year.
Having changed where the calendar began,
the later months with number names were wrong!
But out of respect for old traditions,
the months with number names were just retained,
and kept both their names and their positions.
Though later on two of them were re-named,
all of the months from September onwards
are still known by old numbers, out of place.
That's why the name of month twelve means "Tenth Month."
Here's wishing you a joyous December!

Rosa Parks Day
12-1-20.ii

On December 1, thank Rosa Parks
who had the courage to tell someone, "No."
She faced arrest, jail, and prosecution
for sitting in her own seat on the bus.
Can you imagine such segregation
as part of the law, legally enforced?
Just because it's legal, don't mean it's right!
"All people are equal under the law"

is a founding first principle, and true –
that is, it *should* be true, but to our shame
we've failed to live up to our great ideals
over, and over, and over again.
And yet, we continue to fight for them
because we believe in democracy
and the possibilities of freedom.
We believe that someday, if we all fight,
our founding principles will be applied
at last to ev'ryone; no matter who
they are, or how they look, or where they're from,
or who they worship, or how much they earn;
for we are all one, despite diff'rences –
let us celebrate what makes each unique,
rather than trying to crush the others
with discrimination and oppression
that's based on race, gender, or whatever!
There is no excuse for segregation.
Let us all sit together, and be brave:
as brave as Rosa Parks was on that day.

The Twelfth Month
12-3-20

The month we call December nowadays
was on the ancient Hebrew calendar
marked as "Kislev," of lunar months the ninth.

But just next door in ancient Egypt, they
a solar calendar had, just like us:
and on it, the fourth month was named "Choiac" –
more research I'd needs do to explain more.

The ancient calendars of Macedon,
birthplace of Alexander scourge of Greece,
would have labeled this month, "Apellaios,"
perhaps to honor their god, Apollo?
But here I'm speculating once again.

The beautiful calendar of British Isles
(perhaps I'm biased by my love, but still)
denotes this cherished month the month of Yule –
the same name they gave to the next month, too!
(although Bēdē spells the month name "Giuli")
On axis of Solstices turns the year,
and each Solstice shares with its month its name
as well as the next month – yes, twice a year!
The Winter Solstice, year's paramount day,
is cause for celebration, as we know!

The ancient Norse may have called it the same,
my primstav source seems to suggest that's so;
but my translation of Snorri's *Edda*
gives to this time the cold name of "Frost Month."

Repeal Day
12-5-20.iii

December 5 is Repeal Day
when Prohibition finally went away
a-way back when, in 1933,
allowing alcohol to you and me.
The 18th Amendment was reversed
by a new Amendment, the 21st.
We can't outlaw the private things folks do:
our own behavior's up to me and you.

Pearl Harbor Remembrance Day
12-7-20

The country had tried neutral to remain,
for no one really wants to go to war
when fighting is a source of so much pain –
until the bombs fell, and through peace they tore.
The morning of the 7th, a Sunday,
no one suspected a surprise attack!
Unto the chapel sailors went to pray
aboard their ships – but many ne'er came back.
Advantage seized by Japanese Empire
to bomb the Navy that in harbor lay.
Aggression such as this must needs require
a declaration to join in the fray.
Our entry to the World War was begun
in Pearl Harbor on this day, 1941.

Hanukkah Begins
12-11-20

O celebrate the Festival of Lights!
On the menorah, burn the candles bright –
for each day's observance, light one candle more,
rememb'ring everything that's gone before:
the battle won in days of Maccabee
when by the holy oil lamp folks did see.
They thought they had not fuel enough to last,
yet the lamp burned until the feast had passed.
That history Jewish folks celebrate
each year at this time, and it's worth the wait:
for spirits are filled and given a lift
by feasting, and family exchanging gifts,
with latke and dreidel and wise insights
on Hanukkah, the feast that lasts eight nights!

Saturnalia (December 17 to 22)
12-19-20

The Roman Saturnalia festival,
possibly an ancestor of Christmas
lasted for five days: high point of the year!
It was a time of social reversal
when masters sat down to dinner with slaves
and men and women both went cross-dressing.
Public drunkenness was quite expected,
and insubordinate speech was allowed.
Give homage to Saturn, the harvest god
who presided over communism
before the modern gods had yet been born.
To times of plenty, pray we may return!

Yule Eve
12-20-20

Now, as the Earth moves closer to the Sun
begins the coldest time of the whole year
for us, up in the Northern Hemisphere –
seasonal paradox of atmosphere,
and of the planet's tilt on its axis
(more powerful than orbital variance).
Although the tilt is greatest Solstice day,
the atmosphere retains autumnal warmth...
but wintertime grows colder: watch for snow!
The very shortest day of the whole year
is the day on which we say winter starts –
the Winter Solstice, coming tomorrow!

Yule
12-21-20

Winter Solstice, Reason for the Season,
the shortest day of the year is today!
We celebrate because this day will mark
a turning point, for the days grow longer
after this day, and with the Sun comes hope.
Tomorrow will be brighter than today,
even if it's cloudy and raining hard:
we know that it will be a long journey,
but we have turned a corner once again
t'wards summer we are now on the long path back.

Indeed, this time of year has been a cause
for celebration in many cultures
for thousands of years, throughout distant time.
The ancient Druids constructed Stonehenge
upon the Wiltshire plains in South England
perhaps four or five thousand years ago.
Great megalithic stones they did align
so through them Solstice sunset light would shine.
And likewise, ancient Newgrange in Ireland
and Maeshowe in Orkney were both aligned
with beams of rising Winter Solstice sun.
The Roman Saturnalia at this time
was clearly celebrating Solstice-tide.
In ancient Persia, Yalda was the name
of the night when light won its great vict'ry
defeating darkness, and with it, evil!
They served watermelon and pomegranate
at fam'ly gatherings to celebrate
and read the poetry of great Hafiz.
The Norse, of course, would celebrate the Juul:
short days were quite noticeable to them!
They would burn a traditional Yule log
as I described in my old Pagan book.

The ancient Incas, once a world power,
paid homage to their sun god on this day.
The celebrations, outlawed by Catholics,
have been revived in modern-day Peru
and Guatemala, where people pole-dance
invoking the return of the sunlight.

Christmas Eve
12-24-20

On Christmas Eve we pray to Santa Claus
to bring us lots of gifts, shiny and new,
that in the morn our stockings will be filled
with novelties and goodies, toys and treats!
This mythic figure has a pantheon
of magic beings who all work for him:
there's Dasher and Dancer, Prancer, Vixen,
and Comet, Cupid, Donder, and Blitzen,
and of course Rudolph with his bright red nose,
those flying reindeer pull his magic sleigh;
a workshop full of elves who work all year
for very little pay and lesser fame
in workshops with no safety standards near,
we do not know a single one by name!
And of course, the North Pole is graced by she
who's really in charge of the whole shebang.
Although again we don't know her first name,
good Mrs. Claus is totally in charge
and Santa just does her bidding each year,
as down the chimney he fits his belly,
a miracle modern physics defies!

Christmas Day
December 25

You don't have to believe in Virgin Birth
or magic star that guided Three Wise Men
to offer up a prayer for Peace on Earth
and love to fam'ly'n friends from way back when!
The caroling, the feasting, and the gifts,
the tree, the decorations, and the lights
bring us good cheer and our spirit uplifts
making this day belov'd from morn 'til night.
So strike the chord, and come on, sing along
with one of those old tunes that we all know.
I'm sure you have a fav'rite Chistmas song
about chestnuts, and loved ones, and the snow!
I'm not a member of the faith, it's true,
but I'll wish a Merry Christmas to you!

Boxing Day
12-26-20.ii

In Canada, on Boxing Day,
box old stuff up, and give it away.

The Week of Kwanzaa
12-27-20

Although it's not for me to claim this week
(the celebration's not my heritage)
I'm pleased to name important seven days
of Kwanzaa, celebrated 'cross the land
by African-American people
connecting their culture to days before
their ancestors were brought here on slave ships,
the great shame of our nation's history.

In search of new cultural unity,
Maulana Karenga started Kwanzaa
in 1966, and now it is
by millions of people celebrated
each year, for the week following Christmas.

First is Umoja, day of Unity.
Next is Kujichagulia, important
as the day of Self-Determination.
Ujima celebrates collectivist
ideas of shared responsibility
so foreign to most people in our time.
Ujamaa takes this to the next level
with ideas of a shared economy;
for why should the few keep all the profits
while the many work for next to nothing?
"Let's support local businesses instead!"
Nia is the day of Purpose: "Let's go!"
Kuumba the day of Creativity
challenges folks to "think outside the box."
And finally, Imani is the day
of Faith. "It's possible!" people proclaim.

May Kwanzaa bring your family much joy.

New Year's Eve
January 31

The year draws to a close,
    our thoughts turn to the next;
our feelings at this time,
    hard to set down in text.

As Times Square drops the ball
    we sing our Auld Lang Syne
and count down to the end
    of this grand unit of time.

Draws this year to an end,
    and it's been good, my dear.
Now look we forward to
    an excellent New Year!

the cycle begins anew

Afterword

Hey, did you read all that? That's awesome! *You* are awesome!

If you found this book interesting, then you may also enjoy the companion volumes of poetry composed during that turbulent year:

Choosing Change: Transformational poems of mindset and success. When you're ready for a change, start here.

Poems for the Holidays: An irreverent selection of verses about holiday fun, including Christmas trees, wreaths, stockings, Santa Claus, and more!

The Histories: Poetic short biographies of familiar modern figures told in verse form; the exile of the poet Ovid by the Emperor Augustus; poems about recent events of historical significance; eye-opening notes on cultural traditions, and more!

A Year Outside of Time: A passionate personal perspective on daily life during the world-changing events of 2020 and early 2021.

A Different Thousand and One Nights: Poetic retellings of familiar stories and fairy tales.

Errata

Any factual errors that may be found to be contained within these pages are undoubtedly my own fault, and should not be blamed on my sources.

Regarding Bede: throughout the year's writing and previously, I had always assumed a Greco-Roman pronunciation for the venerable monk's name, with a long vowel for the final "e." That is, I had always pronounced his name Bēdē, that is, "bee-dee," like the noise made by the robot sidekick in *Buck Rogers.* It turns out, most people pronounce the monk's name "Beed." Whoops, my mistake! Rather than rewrite the poems to fit the proper pronunciation, I used an accent symbol over the vowels to indicate my deviant pronunciation. I hope the serious scholars will forgive me, if they ever read any of this.

References and Resources

I referenced a number of Wikipedia entries: including articles relating to modern holidays; the structure of the modern calendar; the month names of various ancient cultures; Greco-Roman gods and goddesses; historical events; and biographies of historical persons. For current events, my primary news source is the CNN mobile app, although I have also referenced The Guardian, NPR, The Oregonian, The Statesman-Journal, The Daily Show, and a variety of less reputable sources via social media.

I gratefully referenced the following resources:

Bede. (trans, ed, intro, notes & commentary by Faith Wallis). (2012 ed). *Bede: The Reckoning of Time, Translated with introduction, notes and commentary by Faith Wallis.* Translated Texts for Historians, Volume 29. Liverpool, UK: Liverpool University Press.

Chabad-Lubavitch Media Center. (2023). *Jewish Holidays.* Retrieved September 29, 2023 from https://www.chabad.org/holidays/default_cdo/jewish/holidays.htm

Eratosthenes and Hyginus. (Robin Hard, trans., introd. & notes). (2015). *Constellation Myths with Aratus's Phaenomena.* Oxford, UK: Oxford University Press (Oxford World's Classics).

Frost, Robert. (1969 ed.) *The Poetry of Robert Frost: Edited by Edward Connery Lathem.* New York: Holt, Rinehart and Winston.

History.com Editors. (Last updated September 26, 2023). *Cesar Chavez.* Retrieved September 29, 2023 from https://www.history.com/topics/hispanic-history/cesar-chavez

Kirton, Sarah. (2002) *Primstav – an ancient calendar form – The Fall Months.* Retrieved from https://norcalspelmanslag.org/ncsnlf2002/ncsnlf2002b.html

Lucretius. (Ronald Melville, trans.). (2008 ed.). *On the Nature of the Universe: A verse translation by Ronald Melville, with an Introduction and Notes by Don and Peta Fowler.* Oxford, UK: Oxford University Press (Oxford World's Classics).

Macphail, Cameron. (December 21, 2020). "Winter Solstice 2020: Why do Pagans celebrate the shortest day of the year?" *The Telegraph.* Retrieved from https://www.telegraph.co.uk/christmas/2020/12/21/winter-solstice-2020-december-shortest-day-year-what-means/

Maudslay, Francesca (director). (2010). *When Rome Ruled: War Machine.* National Geographic Television, DVD. Universal City, CA: Vivendi Entertainment (Distributor).

Ovid. (Anne & Peter Wiseman, trans, ed, & notes). (2013 ed.). *Fasti.* Oxford, UK: Oxford University Press (Oxford World's Classics).

Ovid. (trans. A.D. Melville, intro & notes E.J. Kenney; translation of "The Art of Love" by B. P. Moore with revisions by A.D. Melville). (2008 ed.) *The Love Poems.* Oxford, UK: Oxford University Press (Oxford World's Classics). [This rhyming verse translation includes all of Ovid's famous transgressive works of "love" poetry, for which he was later exiled: *Amores, Cosmetics for Ladies, Ars Amatoria,* and *Remedia Amatoria.*]

Ovid. (trans, ed, intro & notes Peter Green). (2005 ed.). *The Poems of Exile: Tristia and the Black Sea Letters, With a New Foreword; Translated with an Introduction, Notes, and Glossary by Peter Green.* Berkeley, CA: University of California Press.

Smith, Jesse S. (2016 ed.). *Rise of the Pagans.* Silverton, Oregon: Basementia Publications.

Stillman, Janice (editor). (2020). *The Old Farmer's Almanac: 2021.* The Old Farmer's Almanac, No. 229. Dublin, OH: Yankee Publishing, Inc.

[Used to identify event dates which will become the topics of poems in early 2021.]

Sturluson, Snorri (author); Byock, Jesse L. (translation & introduction). (2005 ed.) *The Prose Edda.* New York, NY: Penguin Classics (Penguin Group (USA) Inc.).

Zoll, Kenneth J. (2008). *Sinagua Sunwatchers: An Archaeoastronomy Survey of the Sacred Mountain Basin.* Sedona, AZ: Sunwatcher Publishing.

www.ingramcontent.com/pod-product-compliance
Lightning Source LLC
Chambersburg PA
CBHW021632120626
46545CB00002B/503